Python Coding

Step-by-step beginners' guide to learning python programming language with hands-on project. Exercises included.

Zed Fast

Table of Contents

Introduction

Congratulations on purchasing *Python Coding* and thank you for doing so. With the world becoming more digital and technology affecting each sector separately, so is programming. Programming is one of the essential elements in creating different computer languages and requires varying degrees of skills to develop a functional programming language. Python programming is one of the high-level and well-interpreted languages emphasizing on code readability. For beginners, Python programming may seem like a typical technique when coding and writing clearly despite some dissimilarity. However, beginners may face a challenge when working with Python programming.

The following chapters, therefore, provide crucial information on Python programming, especially for beginners. The first step the book highlights understands what Python programming is all about and the general concept of what you need. In some cases, programmers may miss some vital knowledge concerning Python programming. Henceforth, the following chapters precisely detail everything you need to know about Python programming. The guide is suitable for both programmers and learners who can implement the information provided immediately for use.

With learning about Python programming out of the way, you will understand the benefits of using the language and a step-by-step guide on understanding how to maneuver in various sections. The book also rounds up several aspects, including downloading and installation of the Python as well as a guide on creating your first Python program. With different versions since its incorporation, Python programming supports different programming paradigms, for instance, procedural will be discussed later in the chapters.

There are plenty of books on this subject on the market, thanks again for choosing this one! Every effort was made to ensure it is full of as much useful information as possible, please enjoy it!

Chapter 1: Introduction to Python Coding

Python is one of the most powerful and multi-purpose programming languages. It was created by Guido van Rossum who continues to work towards its advancement. Python language is elementary and ideal for people who are willing to learn computer programming. Its syntax is easy-to-use and can be easily understood.

Getting Started with Python

In this section, we are going to discuss how one can install and run Python on their computers. Learning the two activities can help one in writing their first Python program appropriately.

As a cross-platform programming language, Python can run on numerous platforms. It can run on macOS, Linux, and Windows. Python has also ported to the NET and Java virtual machines. The porting has been possible because it is free and open-source. It is, however, important to always consider installing the most current version of Python in Mac and Linux. Upgrading helps in eliminating cases of using out-of-date Python.

One easy way to run Python is through the use of Thonny IDE. Thonny IDE comes bundled with the latest version of Python. It saves programmers the task of having to install Python separately. The following are some of the simplest steps you can follow when running Python on your machine.

1. Downloading Thonny IDE.

2. Running the installer to help in installing Thonny on the computer.

3. Go to File > New. At this point, save the file with .py extension. For instance, "example.py, good.py" You can as well assign any name to the file. However, make sure that the name ends with ".py"

4. Write the Python code within the file and then save it.

5. The last step involves going to Run> Run the current script. You can also click on F5 to run Python.

Installing Python Separately

There are instances where you may not want to use Thonny when installing and running Python on your computer. The following are the steps that you can follow.

1. Download the latest Python version.

2. Run an installer file and follow each step to install Python.

During the process of installation, check "Add Python to environment variables". This will help in adding Python to environment variables. It will also enable you to run Python from any section of your computer. You can as well select the path through which Python is installed. Once the installation process is done, the Python can run.

1. Run Python in Immediate Mode

After installing Python, typing it in the command line will lead to invoking the interpreter in the immediate mode. Python code can be directly typed, and enter is pressed to bring about the output. For example, when one types 1+1 and then presses enter, the output will be 2. The prompt can be applied as a calculator. When exiting the mode, you should type "quit ()" and then press enter.

2. Run Python in the Integrated Development Environment

A programmer can apply text editing software when writing Python script files. The most essential thing to do is to save the text with the ".py" extension. Using an integrated development environment can make your life as a programmer much easier. It comes in the form of software that serves the purpose of providing useful features to Python. Such features include syntax checking and highlighting, file explorers, and code hinting to help the programmer in the development of applications.

When Python is installed, IDLE, which is an IDE name, is installed as well. It is used when running Python on the computer. It is considered as a decent IDE for use by beginners. Opening IDLE also opens the Python Shell. After this is done, a programmer can create and save new files with ".py" extension.

The First Python Program

After installing and running Python, it is now possible for you to write the first Python program. You can do this by creating a simple program named "Hello Mister!" The program is simple, and its output will be Hello Mister! displayed on the screen. The simplicity of the Python program makes it useful when introducing new programming languages to beginners. The beauty of Python programming language is its ease-of-use and understanding.

Python Programming Keywords and Identifiers

In this part, you will learn on the reserved words in Python and the names that are given functions and variables. Keywords are referred to as reserved words because a name cannot be used as a name, function, Variable, or other identifiers. Keywords are used in defining the structure and syntax of the Python language. Keywords used in Python programming are case sensitive.

There are over thirty keywords used in Python 3.7. The number of keywords can, however, vary over time. All the keywords used in Python are in lowercase except True, False, and None. The keywords must be written as they are.

Keywords in Python

False class finally is

None continue for lambd

True def from nonlo

and del global not

as elif if or

 assert else pass import

break except in raise

It may be quite overwhelming to look at all the keywords simultaneously. All the keywords above may be altered in the different Python versions. Something extra may be added to the keywords, or some may be removed from the keyword.

True, False Keywords

These are considered as the truth values in Python. They are the outcomes of logical or Boolean operations and comparison operations. When the operations are true, the interpreter returns True; and when they are not, it returns False.

None

The keyword None is seen as a unique constant in Python programming. It is used in representing a null value or the absence of the value. None is an object having its data type, referred to as the NoneType. Multiple None objects cannot be created, but it can be assigned to variables. The variables will, in turn, be equal to each other. When applying the keyword None, one should be very careful to avoid False implications, or empty dictionary, string, or list. Void functions do not return anything but automatically return a None object. Anytime a program flow fails to encounter return statements. It also gives the outcome as None.

and, or, not

These are considered as the logical operators used in Python. *and* gives an outcome of True only when both operations are True. *or* gives an outcome of true when any of the operands is True. *not* keyword is used when inverting the truth value.

as

The keyword "as" is used when creating an alias when modules are being imported. It means assigning different user-defined names to modules when they are being imported.

assert

The keyword is used in the process of debugging. assert helps programmers to check on the internal states. It also helps in determining whether the assumptions made are true. It allows programmers to perform the two tasks and conveniently find bugs. A condition should follow the assert keyword. When the condition is true, there is nothing that happens. When it is false, AssertionError is given as the outcome.

break, continue

The keywords are used within loops to allow alteration in their normal behavior by loops. The break helps in ending the smallest loops within. It also controls the flow to the statements directly below the loop. Continue, on the other hand, leads to an end in the current iteration in the loop. It does not affect the entire loop.

def

The keyword def is used when defining user-defined functions.

del

It is used when deleting the references to Python objects.

Python Identifiers

Identifiers are the names given to entities such as variables, functions, and class. They help in differentiating entities from each other. Some rules should be followed when writing identifiers.

1. Identifiers can be written as combinations of letters in uppercase (A-Z) or lowercase (a-z). They can also be underscores (names) or digits (0-9).

2. Python identifiers should not start with digits. For instance, 2variable is seen as invalid, whereas variable2 is perfect.

3. Keywords should not be used as Python identifiers.

4. Special symbols such as @, $,! and % cannot be used together with Python identifiers.

5. Python identifiers can be of any length.

Important Things to Remember

Python is one of the most case-sensitive languages used in programming today. It means that Variable and Variable are different words. It is vital to name identifiers that make sense.

C=10 is valid, but count= 10 can make more sense. It makes it easier for a person reading the code to understand its work.

An underscore also referred to as a long variable, can be used in separating multiple words.

Python Statement, Indentation, and Comments

Python Statement: Statements are the instructions that can be executed by a Python interpreter. For instance, a=1 is termed as an assignment statement. The for statement, while statement, or if statement are other statements used in Python.

Multi-line statement

A newline character is used in marking the end of a Python statement. Statements can, however, be made to extend over several lines. These lines usually have a line continuation character as the "/". The continuation of a line in Python is usually enclosed inside parentheses, braces, and brackets.

Python Indentation

Most of the programming languages such as Java, C, and C++ assign braces when defining blocks of code. Python, however, uses indentation. A code block is the body of a loop or function in programming. In Python, the code block begins with indentation and ends with a line that is unindented. The amount of indentation used depends on the preference of the programmer. Indentation should, however, be consistent all through the block. Basically, four whitespaces are applied in the indentation.

Enforcing indentation in Python makes the code appear uncluttered and clean. During line continuation, the indentation can be ignored. It is, however, an essential idea to indent code to make it readable.

Python Comments

Python comments are critical when Python programs are being written. The comments give descriptions of the activities that are taking place inside a program. They help programmers looking for the source code to understand it more easily and precisely. Explaining the concepts through the use of comments can help a program to be more productive. Comments are useful in instances where one forgets to write the details of programs that they wrote earlier.

When writing a comment, the hash sign is used to indicate its beginning. The hash symbol creates an extension to the newline character. Comments are used by programmers to promote a better understanding of Python programs. Interpreters in Python ignore the comments.

Multi-line comments exist when comments have extended multiple lines. The hash symbol is used in such cases to show the beginning of each line. Triple quotes can also be used in multi-line comments. They are generally used in multi-line strings. When used in multi-comments, they should not generate extra codes.

Docstrings in Python

Docstring is a term used to represent documentation string. It is a type of Python string occurring as the initial statement in a program, class, method definition, or class. It is vital to write things that class and function do within the docstring. Triple quotes are applied anytime docstrings are being written. Docstring is assigned to a programmer in the form of the attribute_ doc_ belonging to the function.

Python Variables

Python variables are named locations used in storing data within the memory. It makes sense to look at Python variables as containers holding data that can be altered later through the entire programming. Variables can also be seen as bags used in storing books, and the books can be replaced anytime. In Python programming, the assignment operator "=" is used when assigning values to the variables. It is also possible for a single value to be assigned to multiple variables simultaneously.

Constants

Constants are types of Python variables whose values cannot be altered. Constants on Python can be seen as the containers holding information that cannot be transformed later. Basically, we can view them as bags where books have been stored, and once placed in the bag, the books cannot be replaced.

Assigning and declaring values to constants are made on a module. In this case, the module is the new file that contains variables, classes, and functions. It is later imported to the main file. Constants inside the modules are written in capital letters. Underscores are used to separate the words.

Rules and Naming Convention for Constants and Variables

1. Names assigned to variables and constants should comprise of letters in uppercase or lowercase or underscores or digits.

2. Programmers should create names that make sense. For instance, the example makes some more sense than e.

3. When a programmer wants to create variable names with two words, underscores should be used when separating them.

4. When possible, capital letters should be used when declaring constants.

5. Special symbols such as ! @, $, or % should never be used.

6. A variable name should never be started with a digit.

Literals

Literals are raw data assigned in constants or variables. There are various types of literals available in Python programming. The Numeric laterals are unchangeable or immutable. They belong to three varied numerical types Float, Complex, and Integer. String literals are defined as patterns of characters that are surrounded by quotes. Python programmers can effectively use either single, double, or triple quotes for each string. And is a character literal in the form of a single character that is surrounded by one or double-quotes. Boolean literals usually have either the True or False values. Special literals typically comprise of None. It is the only special literal in Python and is used in specifying fields that are not created.

Python Data Types

All values in Python usually have data types. Data types are present because everything in Python is considered an object. They can be defined as variables and classes. There are numerous data types in Python programming. In this section, we shall discuss the most important ones.

1. Python Numbers

Floating point numbers, complex numbers, and integers all fall under the Python Numbers data type. Their definitions are given as float, complex, and int in Python. The type () function is used in identifying the class to which a value or Variable belongs to. The isinstance () function is used when checking whether objects belong to particular classes. The limitation to the length of integers is only brought about by the available memory.

Floating-point numbers are accurate up to 15 decimal places. Decimal points are used when separating floating points and integers. In this case, 2 is an integer, and 2.0 is a floating-point number. Compound numbers in Python are written as "x + y". X is the true part, whereas y is an imaginary part.

2. Python List

A list is an ordered pattern of elements. Python list data type is very flexible, thus being the most commonly used data type. The Declaration of Python lists is very simple. The simplicity is because commas are used when separating items, and all are enclosed in brackets. The slicing operator is used when extracting one or multiple items from a Python list. Indexes in Python programming starts from 0. Lists in Python are mutable. It means that the value of items in the Python list can be changed with time.

3. Python Tuple

Python tuple is a data type that is defined as an ordered pattern of items similar to the Python list. The difference between the two is that Python tuples are immutable. This means once they are created, modification is not possible. Python tuples are used when writing-protect data. Their speed is higher than that of the lists because they cannot be dynamically changed. The definition of a Python tuple is enclosed within parentheses. Commas separate items in the tuple. Similar to the Python list, the slicing operator is also used when extracting items from the Python tuple. However, the value of the elements being extracted cannot be changed.

4. Python Strings

Strings are sequences of Unicode elements. Single or double quotes can be used in representing strings. Triple quotes, on the other hand, are used when denoting multi-line strings. Similar to Python tuple and list, the slicing operator is used when extracting items from strings. Strings are also unchangeable. It means that even after elements are extracted, their value does not change.

5. Python Set

Set is an unordered grouping of unique elements. Python set is described by the use of values that are separated by commas. The values are all enclosed within braces. The elements of a set do not have a specified order. The unique values in sets help in eliminating duplicates. The operations in a set can be performed in the form of a union, intersecting between two sets. Due to their unordered grouping, indexing is not useful. The slicing operator can, therefore, not work in the Python set.

6. Python Dictionary

A Python dictionary is a group of key-value pairs that do not have an order. The dictionary is commonly used when there are vast amounts of data to be dealt with. They are optimized to help in easier data retrieving. For a programmer to effectively retrieve data, they should identify the key. Braces are used when defining dictionaries in Python. Every item in the dictionary is in the form of a pair appearing as a key: value. The key and the value are of any form.

Conversion between Data Types

Python provides an opportunity for programmers to convert between various data types. It is possible through the use different type conversion functions such as str(), float(), and int(). Conversions from float to int truncates the values. Truncate means that the value is brought closer to zero. When converting between strings, the values contained in it must be compatible. When they are not, it results in an error. It is also possible to convert a sequence to another. When converting to a dictionary, every element in the group must occur as a pair.

Chapter 2: Python Interpreters

Python, as a programming language, has major roles in the field of programming. For instance, Python is used in:

- Graphical User Interface in desktops

- Web application and frameworks

- OS

- Development of languages

- Prototyping

Python is highly regarded to its diverse advantages that create an impressive environment for the programmers. Basically, there are two classifications of programming languages. A high-level language refers to the language that human being understands. Low-level language refers to the language that a computer understands. An interpreter translates the high-level language into an executable form.

Python is a programming language; however, there is always a difference in the language understood by the computer and the one used by man. Therefore, to ensure that the intended activity will happen, each programming language has an interpreter. An interpreter is a computer program that aids the execution of the instruction in a given coding.

There are several advantages of programming language interpretation, such as:

- It saves on space: An interpreter uses less memory than the files to be executed. This is because only particular source codes are in memory per time.

- An interpreter can be used in debugging: some minor elements in programming such as commas, colons, and the likes can cost the programmer his or her precious time. However, in case of an error, the interpreter prints the message of error as it uses the source codes.

How is Python, being a programming language, interpreted? The answer is simple. The source codes of the program are converted into machine language for execution. Therefore, the main reason for interpreting is to create a union between the programmer and the computer. Equally, most of Python's interpreters are implementations of Python programming language. Therefore, they are advantageous since each implementation in the programming filed is meant to create a solution to a given problem. There are several common Python interpreters, namely:

1. CPython.

2. IronPython.

3. Jython.

4. PyPy.

5. PythonNet.

6. Stackless Python.

1. **CPython**

As the name suggests, it is an implementation of Python language. However, it is written in two languages; C and Python. CPython has been embraced by many programmers, among other implementations of a language. The main difference between Python and CPython is that Python is a language on its own. On the other hand, CPython is an implementation of Python using C language.

However, CPython can be termed as an interpreter, and at the same time, a compiler. As a compiler, the CPython compiles the codes written in Python into byte-code before making the interpretation. Due to the fact of conjoined language, a programmer should be well versed in both C and Python to understand the executions.

There is one unique feature of CPython. In a single process, it is only a single thread that processes the Python byte-code at a go. In order to achieve this feature, CPython uses the Global Interpreter Lock (GIL). That notwithstanding, there can be cases of multithreading which occurs when the particulate thread is in wait of an external process to complete.

For instance, when there are three clients to be served by threads, multithreading will have to occur. For instance, a single thread may be waiting for the reply from the client, the second waiting for execution of the query by the database, while the third may be the one actively processing Python code. However, the GIL does mean that CPython is not suitable for processes that implement CPU intensive algorithms in Python code that could potentially be distributed across multiple cores.

In the world of programming, the cases of interference of GIL are rare. The reason being Python language is known to be a slow language and, therefore, cannot be used in the CPU-intensive activities. Such activities include the processing of images and neural networks. As a result, Python language is used in artificial levels, and the call functions in the libraries perform specialized tasks. The libraries are usually not coded in Python; therefore, a Python code in a different thread cannot be halted while a call to one of these processes takes place. Since the Python library is subjected to GIL, the non-Python library is preferred for CPU-intensive tasks. This is because it can simultaneously execute multiple threads on multiple processors without hindrances.

For Python code to be executed simultaneously, the CPython interpreter is involved in multitasking by the operating system. However, this situation interferes with the communication between the simultaneous Python processes; that notwithstanding, the multiprocessing module lessens the interference. As a result, applications can benefit from the simultaneous execution of Python code, and at the same time, be implemented with a limited amount of overhead.

Implementation of CPython is made easier by the presence of GIL; therefore, it is easier to perform a multi-thread application that does not rely on the simultaneous execution of the Python code. In the absence of GIL, the multiprocessor must ensure the codes are safe.

Though many programmers have objected to the elimination of GIL, it has been argued out that the advantages of GIL outweigh its disadvantages.

Unladen Swallow

Unladen Swallow was an improvement of CPython, and it was supposed to be totally compatible and considerably quicker. It aimed to attain its goals by supplementing the customs of the CPython virtual machine with a timely compiler engineered using LLVM. The project had the primary goal of a speed improvement; however, this goal was not met.

The project was owned by Thomas Wouters, Jeffrey Yasskin, and Collin Winter, who by then were an employee of Google. Despite Google sponsoring the project, most of the stakeholders were not members of Google fraternity. The codes of Unladen Swallow were hosted on the Google Code.

Despite the lack of attaining the primary goal, Unladen Swallow achieved the goal of adding code to the main Python implementation. Such achievements include the cPickle module.

2. **IronPython**

IronPython is an interpreter which resulted from an implementation of the Python programming language. The implementation targeted the .NET framework and the Mono. The pioneer of this project was Jim Hugunin, and he was consistent until version 1.0 was developed. This version was released on the fifth of September 2006. The development proceeded even in his absence, and version 2.0 was later released on the tenth of December, 2008. The version was managed, and a team from Microsoft until version 2.7 beta 1 was released. However, the project was abandoned by Microsoft as Hugunin got hired by Google. Since then, the project is managed by GitHub, voluntarily. IronPython is now a free and open-source application and can work with other Python Tools and can be alternated with Visual Studio, which is also a free and open-source application and an extension of Visual Studio IDE hosted by Microsoft.

IronPython is programmed using C#; however, there is the inclusion of Python code, which is automatically generated by a code generator in Python. IronPython is used superficially on the Dynamic Language Runtime (DLR). DLR is a library that operates superficially on the

Common Language Infrastructure. DLR provides typing and method dispatch, which are dynamic alongside the dynamic languages. DLR is a component of .NET 4.0 and Mono; it is used as a library on former CLI implementations.

In case of an error, IronPython interprets it and prints and stack trace. The main difference between IronPython and Python is that Python is a language, while IronPython is its implementation. Of equal importance, IronPython is designed to work in CLR, which is .NET Framework making it more viable to programmers who use .NET.

Advantages of Using IronPython

- It has an extensibility layer to application software in its function, written in the .NET language.

- It is easy to comprehend the IronPython.

- It can be integrated with the .NET application framework.

- After development, the developers can associate easily with the script written in IronPython.

- It interacts freely with .NET objects in the framework.

- It has an extended interface of functionality framework; hence, one does not have to change any of the codebases of the framework.

- When passed in reference to a .NET object, it imports the types and methods availed by that object, automatically.

- The .NET libraries are available.

- It has an impressive user interface. The user-friendly interface is meant to boost usability.

- It accommodates the components of the third party like Essential Grid of Syncfusion without the interference of the performance.

- A graphical user interface can be developed using Visual Studio, and the dialog designed using C#, and the behavior of the interface designed using IronPython.

- In case of error, the CLR debugger works well to save the programmer's time. Equally, the debugger will help in articulating and generation of possible hindrances of successful application development. This will, in turn, help in the enlightenment of the programmer.

The disadvantage of IronPython verse using C#

- The start-up time is prolonged, making it slow. However, the developers are working to solve this, but currently, it is a problem. Therefore, hopefully, the next implementation or development of the buffering during the initiation of a program will be addressed.

- There is no developed Language Integrated Query.

- If your priority is IP, you should know that dynamic languages do not have time to compile and perform health checks on your codebase, so problems that occur at runtime. When writing the test code for the first time, the impact is less. However, if you do not write a solid amount of test code, then you may want to use a language that is statically typed.

The disadvantages of IronPython verse CPython

- A cross-platform is not present. The only available compatible platform is that of Windows. Therefore, there has been an urge to create features that are supportive and compatible with Linux and Mac. The explanation for this is that many third-parties of .NET modules, such as the Synfusion network, are not entirely .NET; for some operations, they fall into win32. Perhaps, this is due to performance issues. This means that your application will not run on platforms other than Windows .NET if you use them.

- There are several CPython C extensions, such as numpy, which is a library of numeric functions. As a result, the programmer has to use an open-source library that joins C extensions to IronPython; however, this makes the programming tougher.

Compared to CPython, the reference implementation of Python, the performance and properties of IronPython, is largely dependent on the exact benchmark used. In most benchmarks taken with PyStone, IronPython works worse than CPython but better than other benchmarks. The better IronPython can work for Python's thread or multiple core programs since the JIT is available, and because the Global Interpreter Lock is not provided.

3. **Jython**

From its development, it has been referred to as JPython until 1999. Jython is a complement of Python and Java. It is programmed using Python but can also work on the Java platform. The Jython programs can import and use any class of Java. As a result, Jython programs, save for some standard modules, use Java classes rather than Python modules. In the generic Python programming language distribution, Jython contains almost all modules, which only lack some modules originally implemented in C.

While Python is an extremely powerful programming language that is object-oriented, Jython, as an implementation, is much advantageous as its scripting language can run on JVM.

For instance, Swing, AWT, or SWT can write a user interface in Jython. Jython does the compilation two major modes, namely, on request and statically Java byte-code (the intermediate language).

By the end of 1997, Jython was intentionally modified to replace C with Java for high-performance code accessed by Python programs. A grant was awarded in January 2005 by the Python Software Foundation. In June 2009, Jython 2.5 had been released

Advantages of Using Jython

Python is a scripting language for general purposes; it is also object-oriented. It is a well-known and popular language because it offers high productivity and, consequently, a competitive advantage. It also has a basic syntax that allows the code to be readable (comprehended) and maintained in an easier way.

The language itself has most of the structures and features you might possibly expect, such as objects and functions (methods). The most appealing feature of C or Java to any programmer is arguably the ease with which lists and sequences of values can be created and handled. Together with languages such as mapping and filtering functional programming, it is a very powerful core language.

4. **Pypy**

PyPy is the alternative to CPython programming. Therefore, it is considered to be a standard implementation of the Python programming language. The efficiency, in terms of speed, of PyPyexceeds that of the CPython because PyPy uses the just-in-time concept compiler. Some Python code is PyPy-friendly except for the codes that are dependent on CPython extensions, which do not or do overhead while running in PyPy. Internally, PyPy uses a technique called meta-tracing to transform an interpreter into a just-in-time compiler for tracing. Since it is usually easier for interpreters to write than compilers, this technique can facilitate efficient programming language implementation. However, the launching is relatively slower. RPython is considered a PyPy meta-translation toolchain.

PyPy was developed as implementation or improvement of Python programming language and, therefore, was written in a programming language similar to that of Python. As a result, it is easy to identify the areas for improvements, thus, making PyPy more versatile and simpler than CPython in terms of usability.

PyPy is committed to providing a common framework for the interpretation and support of dynamic language implementation, stressing the clear distinction between language and implementation issues. PyPy also aims to implement the programming language of Python in a compatible, versatile, and speedy manner. Through this implementation, PyPy gives a possibility for new advanced features without encoding low-level information.

The PyPy interpreter is written itself in a small Python subset called RPython. That notwithstanding, RPython presents certain limitations in the Python language so that at the time of compilation, the variable type can be inferred.

The Project PyPy created a toolchain which analyzes the RPython software in tandem with a parser in the C programing language and converts it into a byte code type. Much of this is added to the machine code, and the byte code is compiled and executed by the interpreter.

PyPy interpreter provides plug-in trash collectors as well as Stackless Python features, although it is optional. Finally, there are several annotations in the interpreter's source code, a just-in-time (JIT) generator that creates an only-in-time compiler into the interpreter. The JIT compiler created is a JIT tracker.

RPython is currently also used to write non-Python languages, such as Pixie.

Advantages of using PyPy

- Most of the programmers will love and recommend programs that are not sluggish. PyPy provides that by being faster courtesy of the JIT compiler. Some programmers would argue that interpreters may cause sluggishness of an operation. However, it is not the case with PyPy.

- The compatibility of a program to another can limit the task achieved through programming. However, PyPy is a compatible implementation of

Python language. The compatibility with the original language means that all the features of Python are available with additional one included.

- The storage performance can affect the entire operations of a system. PyPy programs use relatively less space compared to CPython. The less use of space helps in reducing the latency and hence increasing the efficiency.

- The compatibility with other Python libraries makes PyPy more efficient. PyPy is compatible with Python libraries, such as Twisted and Django. The compatibility helps the programmer to insert many desired features in an application using the preferable and compatible language.

- PyPy provides micro-threads concurrency as it can be supported by the stackless mode by default. Concurrency of execution helps in increasing efficiency in terms of speed and latency.

5. **Stackless Python**

Stackless Python is a Python language programming translator. The name stackless means that it averts its stack; however, it relies on C call stack. The Stackless Python functions on the basis of the C stack;

nevertheless, it is clear from function calls. The main feature of stackless Python is that the micro threads are not associated with normal operating system threads. The Stackless adds support for coroutines, communication channels, and serialization of tasks as well as Python features. The programs that run with Stackless Python are usually divided into micro-threads. These threads are managed from the linguistic interpreter but not the kernel of the OS. Therefore, it is the interpreter that manages the context ad tasks.

The Micro-threads are responsible for executing various subtasks in the same CPU core program. They, therefore, serve to avoid the overhead of using separated threads for one-core programs as an alternative to event-based, asynchronous programming. For instance, switching between the Modes, particularly the User and Kernel, is not essential; resultantly, it reduces the Central Processing Unit usage.

While micro-threads ease the tasks by working on a single-core, Stackless Python will not remove Python's GDL lock or use multiple threads and/ or the processes. The stackless only allows cooperative multitasking on a common CPU and not in parallel (pre-empting were not initially available but are lately available, although with some limitations). If you are to use several CPU cores, the communication between the processor's components and the system needs to be built in addition to Stackless Python processes.

However, Stackless Python cannot be installed on an already existing Python application as an extension or a library. This limitation is due to the significant number of changes in the source. Actually, it is a complete distribution of Python itself. Most of the Stackless Python has been implemented in PyPy, an interpreter hosted automatically by Python and JIT compiler. While the entire Stackless is a separate release, it has been effectively bundled as a green-let-based CPython extension. This means that it is used for a green threading solution for CPython by a number of libraries. (e.g., gevent). Since then, Python has a native green thread solution - await / async. Stackless is commonly used to build a massively multiplayer online game for Eve Online and the mail service of IronPort.

Advantages of Using Stackless Python

Stackless Python is an updated programming version of Python. Therefore, it is based on making Python programming more efficient. Among its recommendable features is that the programmer is able to achieve the advantage of thread-based programming without the complexity of normal threads and quality. Equally, the micro-threads of Stackless Python are simple ad lightweight. As a result, it presents the following advantages. First, it increases the structural features of the system. Secondly, the codes are easy to read and comprehend to the programmer. Third, due to efficiency, it boosts the productivity of the programmer.

Chapter 3: Python Compilers

A Python compiler is described as a computer program responsible for translating codes written in one language of programming to another. Python is one of the fastest-growing programming languages in the world. It means that there can be no scarcity when it comes to the Python compilers that can work with different projects. From the definition given earlier, compilers are the programs responsible for converting a source code that is written in the complex language of programming to a more straightforward language like the machine code, which as most of us know, is suitable for creating programs that can be executed.

In this section, we discuss the existing Python compilers and list the best in the business. Later on, we shall also discuss the best Python interpreters and how you can use then. It will help you establish the best use cases for each of the mentioned compiler or interpreter. Additionally, we will also give information on where you can get them from, be it online or manual, and where you can use them without necessarily installing it. More importantly, this article will list some of the advantages or disadvantages of each item where possible.

Well, let's get it started! Not every tool is available on the internet for trial. A good number of compilers require you to install them on your system first before using them. Others can be directly downloaded and connected on your order directly from the internet, while a few others can be downloaded and installed directly from the Windows directory without the need to install the system. The remaining types of compilers can be tested and tried on online platforms and in the browser directly. Most of the compilers discussed in this section are applied in the day-to-day life of a programmer.

Research has shown that the following ten Python compilers are among the best in the field, given they are better in efficiency and delivery. There is a possibility that not every Python program is achieved in all the available databases. This is because each one of them brings on board a specific aspect into play — considering that there no reason whatsoever why all the types of compilers are inexistent to perform the same function.

You might be wondering whether these compilers can be acquired free of charge and whether any of them can be used for commercial purposes. You've been waiting for this moment. Here it is, let's look at each one of them in detail! Well, before we start looking at each one of them, you are warned of the surprise mentions and comprehensive learning experience that you are going to achieve from the points below. Additionally, some of these compilers are not that popular because most of them are only applied in certain cases. Regardless, these compilers are still very essential, and knowing they exist will ensure you are well-informed. Below are some of the best Python compilers in the market today.

CPython

There is a reason why I started the list with this compiler. Well, the idea is, this compiler is among the most popular in the world, and it is widely implemented in Python.

It is a default compiler and interpreter that mostly used when installing the Python program on your machine. It is denoted as the C language of programming CPython since it contains a good number of interfaces as new functions and programming languages like the C. This compiler is recommended for Python implementation, especially when you need a simple measure of compliance and compatibility with the standards listed in raw accolades of performance.

Because this is the most used or rather the most popular version of Python languages, it can be noble for us to start this off by first knowing how CPython operates and then move on to other versions of it. You ought to know that CPython consists of exceptions, dynamic typing, modules, and very sophisticated dynamic classes. This compiler enables you to do the following:

Call C and the C+ codes to and from, and direct from a system of Python remotely. It also allows you to combine the source code levels of dispatching to dig into the Python code of your preference and locate efficiency bottlenecks as well as memory leaks.

CPython can also be referred to as the duplicate of Python language of programming, which consequently lets you call back the C functions, allowing the declaration of C data methods in variables. Lastly, this compiler is a free tool available in the open-source license.

Jython

Just as its name implies, this compiler is the implementation of a Python programming language to run the Java Virtual Machine. The statement means that you came to put in use. Java libraries, as well as the other Java perceptions, are found on the applications. Although most of the Python codes are applied in JVM and Jython. There exist different reasons as to why modules are put into use.

Additionally, the significant gaps that are between the code run on the JVM and Python code because it does not work well with the C extensions. This, however, should not be a significant problem because there are very few chances you will use any of the C extensions in the Python program. In case it happens, the remaining program will work correctly. Below are the quick points you need to know about this compiler:

This compiler was first invented in 2001, January, and the most recent version was updated in 2017, July.

The other thing is that Jython assumes the Python code, then compile it to a similar byte code belonging to Java. This explains why a user can juggle in between any system that runs in JVM. This can be explained further by attending the Java lessons talking about Jython.

For us to explicitly mention what Python and Jython can work on, especially those databases involving JVM, we need first to establish whether Jython works with Python or not. To confirm that, it is time you understand that the Jython compiler does not run with JVM. Lastly, the Jython code does work with CPython perfectly, not unless its files don't contain previously used Java libraries.

The IronPython

Having talked about Python's normal distributor in the first two compilers, it is time we discussed the digital networks. You need to know that there exist several Python implementations that are used to operate on frameworks. Such applications are known as IronPython. Below are a few things you need to know about the IronPython:

First, this compiler was discovered in 2006, and the most recent update was released in early 2018.

The other thing you need to know about IronPython is that it documented in a programming language known as the C#.

Additionally, it supports various elements in the REPL scenery, or instead as an interactive console that supports similar topographical compilation. The other essential thing tech users should know about IronPython is that codes written in it are known to be capable of communicating the consular objectives. Just like the way the previous compiler we discussed operates,

IronPython is more of a link that connects the Java universe and the net universe.

The significant advantage of using IronPython over the other existing compilers is that the current developers can put into use the implementations of Python in the suggestive themes with testing and automating command tasks.

Python can be used in various projects, including the construction of embedded web servers located within an app that can be created using an available web of Python frameworks. It is quicker and easier to come up with compilers that are used in hosting a net linked network placed within an application.

Finally, the IronPython compiler is a product of Microsoft, and therefore, operates under the MPL (Microsoft Public License).

The Stackless Python

It is more of just an upgraded or rather an updated version of the primary programming language of Python, which can be introduced to the system and be more beneficial to the micro-threads. This compiler can save a user from the struggle of dealing with unreadable and complex codes that are ever-present in multi-thread programming.

You might be asking yourself if the concepts linked to threats are sophisticated and complex; what about the micro-threads? It is something we all need to understand. For a start, we can refer to micro threading as a type of model based on software that was tiny and light threads built in the inside of various processors. Each core located in the database system is linked to more than one smaller threads that apply the center in the unused part of its body with a simple process of context switching.

Discussed below are some of the quick points we think you know about this compiler known as the Stackless Python:

No matter the newly introduced threads in the language of programming, this compiler is easy to read and does not give you a hard time trying to interpret it.

With this compiler, the general performance of the system will significantly improve without the need to consume a lot of memory because threads are little in size.

This compiler also brings efficiency to the general programming because the little threads need to highlighted and indicated as the task: a code wrapped within a function that is launched in the form of micro yarns. Additionally, this compiler isn't just about database referencing and threads. It is also involved in sophisticated communication links involving micro threads and round table algorithms that are used in scheduling computer monitors as well as the facility of serialization. The micro thread discussed earlier carry massive advantages such that when you opt to isolate the compiler of stackless from your system, you won't need to make changes on the code you created earlier because of the functions associated with this compiler are simple to comprehend.

Brython

This a compiler that has popularly been labeled as the Python 3 implementors for web programming. It is a widely used Python compiler that plays a role in converting the Python code into a more readable and understandable code of JavaScript. Given the fact that it has been adapted from the HTML 5 field of work, this compiler is equipped with interfaces that are key in events and objects. This compiler is a reduction and modifier for the Python browser as well. It helps boost the functioning of different essential things in a system, including the creation of a more straightforward document element and running 3D navigator. Brython compiler works more efficiently when installed in Google Chrome or Firefox browsers. The compiler doesn't only give support to every modern-day browser but mobile web users as well. The compiler is equipped with a console linked to JavaScript that can be applied in the evaluation of executing time frames of a few programs concerning sufficient levels of editing.

According to the person who invented and created Brython compiler, Dr. Pierre Quentel, the compiler is quicker and more efficient when working with Skulpt and Pyoy.js. On some occasions, this compiler is even faster than Python implementors references like the CPython.

This compiler can support almost all Python 3 syntaxes like generators and comprehensions. Brython also gives significant support to various modules that belong to the CPython distributor and faces a vibratory intersect with several events and elements. Also, a number of the most recent support technology like the HTML5/CSS3 is present in this compiler and can also use the most known CSS framework, such as LESS and BootStrap3.

Nuitka

It is another widely used compiler in the programming language. It functions by taking Python codes and links it to the C/C++ codes or executive orders. Nuitka can be applied in the development of stand out links or programs even though a user might have refrained from running the Python language in a machine.

Nuitka, which is a compiler written in a complete Python programming language, allows the use of several libraries linked to Python as well as other extensive modules. Nuitika is a compiler available to various platforms including macOS X, FreeBSD, Windows as well as NetBSD. It is also a product that has been given a license under Apache. It is available to other platforms like the Anaconda and prefers to be linked with existing projects like machine learning and data science.

PyJS

This is among the most used Python compilers in the market today. We have so far talked about different compilers and their advantages. It is now time we discussed the PyJS. If you are a tech user in search of a platform to write your Python code and then implement it through web browsers, this is the compiler you should work for. It plays a significant role in the translation of systems associated with Python to corresponding JavaScript codes to enable them to get executed in a web browser.

There is an essential aspect accompanying the PyJS compiler, and it is accompanied by an AJAX file that takes care of the gaps in between DOM and JavaScript supports for various web browsers. For it generates JS codes that are equivalent, it establishes a rapport among the two robust abstract syntax levels. You ought to know that it is possible to operate on a Python web application using various source codes on standalone apps that run using the desktop module. Additionally, a good number of compilers have already been established and linked with this one making it one of the most complex and advanced compilers in recent times.

Shed Skin Index

A shed skin index refers to a feature that lets you perform a query to retrieve data from a database more efficiently. A typical index contains several relatable specified tables and holds more than one key. Similarly, a table can have a more set of indexes than it was initially built to provide. You should, however, note that keys are mainly based on the columns created by comparing the keys and allocated indexes. By doing so, it is easier to ensure each database contains a similar amount of data value.

Indexes, just like the constraints discussed earlier, can quickly speed up the process of retrieving data. It is, therefore, important to first modify and correct the indexes as required by each table. In smaller databases, missing indexes will not be shown, and you can be assured that once the schedule starts increasing in size, the queries applied will take a longer time to occur.

When working on a set of databases in which the period of operating on them is roughly around eight days to get it done, it will force you to come up with measures that bring down the period to a shorter period. As a way of achieving that, you can choose to run the database through a query plan developer who can benefit both of the new indexes. This had proven to be very efficient because, from an estimated three hundred thousand operations, the procedure will cut it down to only thirty! This can consequently cut down the number of days you had to work on it from eight to just two hours. Therefore, indexes are much more efficient when it comes to boosting the speed of performance.

Skulpit

This a compiler that has popularly been labeled as the Python 3 implementors for web programming. It is a widely used Python compiler that plays a role in converting the Python code into a more readable and understandable code of JavaScript. Given the fact that it has been adapted from the HTML 5 field of work, this compiler is equipped with interfaces that are key in events and objects. This compiler is a reduction and modifier for the Python browser, as well. It helps boost the functioning of different essential things in a system, including the creation of a more straightforward document element and running 3D navigator. The Skulpit compiler works more efficiently when installed in Google Chrome or Firefox browsers. The compiler doesn't only give support to every modern-day browser but mobile web users as well. The compiler is equipped with a console linked to JavaScript that can be applied in the evaluation of executing time frames of a few programs concerning sufficient levels of editing.

Installing Python Compilers and Database Security

When downloading the SQL database files on a Windows computer, you will come across two different kits: the first one on which the systems run containing the Sun Java SDK and the other one that doesn't include the Sun Java SDK. Make sure you are downloading the right file first before installing it. You are welcome to confirm from the upcoming part of this section vital instructions and requirements needed to install the SQL server.

To begin with, the procedure of installing a SQL database mainly depends on one thing: whether or not the Windows system in use doesn't contain the Sun Java SDK. When working on a Windows system with the release 1.5.0_06 or installed later, we have discussed the steps you need to follow more than in this article. Every other method, including the Mac OS and Linux that have no Java SDK, we have also discussed the procedure you need to follow to install it.

Below, we discuss ways you can install the SQL servers on any computer, be it Windows or Linux. Read on to find out!

When you want to be run and install your SQL developer on Windows operating systems, and the Java script involved is more than the standard update 6, you are recommended to implement the following steps.

Start by unzipping the SQL developer file to the folder you have preferred. For instance, it can be C:\Program

Files. On other computers, it can also be referred to as the SQL developer installer. Once you have unzipped the kit containing the SQL developer, it will trigger a folder named the skulpit to be established the installed SQL file formed earlier. It will also result in various folders and data located in the same directory. If you wish to start running this SQL developer, it is recommended you go to the previously installed SQL folder and then click the sqldevlper.exe. File.

Upon clicking, you will be asked to key in the name for your Java file downloaded earlier, then proceed to click the known corresponding file named program files java folds. When the SQL developer database starts operating, you can as well link to a database of your choice by simply right-clicking the connections option in the known connections navigator, then following it up by choosing a new connection model. Similarly, if you had a few exported connections in the database, it is recommended you import those connections and put them into use.

Chapter 4: Python Coding in Details

Python is one of the leading and popular computer programming languages around the world used in the creation of computer programs. As an essential programming tool, Python consists of multiple components, which include compilers. Python compilers are tools that translate codes written in one or more languages. In other words, these are tools that allow the computer to convert complex programming languages source codes into more understandable languages. For example, a Python compiler can be used to translate machine codes written in a specific language such as from Python codes to C/C++.

Since the introduction of Python in the computing world, especially in programming, compilers have become more available to allow room for increased programming language options. Besides, the use of Python compilers rose over time, leading to modifications allowing these functions to be used as static, dynamic, and in Java. Languages can, therefore, be translated across different programming categories such as from Python language to Java to C/C++ depending on the type used. It is also compatible across all operating systems and supported with almost all programming language tools. However, these Python compilers can again become inadequate when used within Python because recent versions of Python use interpreters to translate codes.

With the benefits of Python compilers becoming more reliant by developers, some state that these versions may, at times, lag. The slow performance often arises when running compiled scripts, especially when not using Python interpreters. Developers have, however, suggested ways of speeding up the process, which has henceforth been found useful. Some of these include conducting arithmetic functions outside the loop, lowering codebases, learning your data structure, and having adequate space more so on memory footprints. In the case of Python compiler lagging in program execution, the use of these solutions has proven to play a significant role in its efficiency.

Python Interpreters

As already stated, Python interpreters can be used as an alternative to Python compilers though they might not perform as a dependable code translator. In this case, Python interpreters are bytecodes that represent the actual machine that runs instructions in programming tools without the need for a compiler. Therefore, Python can either use compilers to interpret codes or run them directly when executing programs. Unlike compilers, Python interpreters use parsing source codes to facilitate translation or execute codes explicitly.

The use of interpreters began in 1952 when the first computer programming language was launched and used as compilers. At the time, interpreters only translated low-level languages with the first version referred to as Lisp created by Steve Russell. From its primary function of converting codes, Lisp led to the creation of several computer programs used today in an advanced format. Similarly, Python uses a similar pattern of interpreters but modified to run high-level computer languages with additional features. As such, Python interpreters tend to run programs directly without the use of translation mechanisms.

Interpreters Vs. Compilers

Generally, computer programs are written using high-level computer languages, which are often understood by humans. However, the computer regularly fails to follow these languages but only familiar with computer codes such as 0 and 1. Source codes, therefore, require a translation to machine codes that are made possible by compilers and interpreters. Both compilers and interpreters are used in Python but separately. This is because they function differently when it comes to converting programs written complex languages. That said, there exist differences between these two key Python source code translators.

Means of Program Translation

When it comes to translation, the general program needs to be translated but takes different forms. That is, both compilers and interpreters take different ways of translating the programs but often result in the intended outcome. Interpreters use the technique of translating one statement at a time from the entire data. This allows Python to focus on a single statement when turning codes until when program as the whole is converted. On the other hand, compilers tend to take the whole program and translate it once. Unlike interpreters, compilers begin by scanning the entire program then changes the source codes into machine codes at once.

Time for Source Code Analysis

Before the source is translated into machine codes, it first undergoes analysis preparing the system to engage in transmuting. In Python interpreters, the process of source code analysis often takes very little time, but more time is used on the translation. Compilers often work on the opposite where the tool takes more time on source code analysis but takes less time on the overall execution process. In this case, Python interpreters and compilers differ on both source code analysis and global execution of the programs, with each taking the vice versa of the other process.

Generation of Intermediate Object Codes

During source code transfer and translation, there may arise the creation of multiple codes that are unnecessary to the end result. These codes are referred to as intermediate objects. In Python compilers, there is the creation of intermediate object codes that demand lining, therefore, the need for more space for the storage of these additional variables. However, Python interpreters do not generate any form of intermediate object codes, therefore, they do not demand additional memory. As such, if you are using compilers to translate one computer language to another, then ensure you have adequate memory space to store other variables generated in the form of intermediate object codes.

Need for Debugging

Debugging is a computer programming term meaning the process of locating bugs and mistakes in computer programs and providing solutions to correct errors before the programs are executed. In Python source code translation to machine codes, there are instances where errors may arise when using either interpreters or compilers. If, for example, you are using an interpreter to translate codes, you may experience a mistake. In this case, the translation process will halt when it meets the error allowing for the debugging process to correct the problem. When using compilers, on the contrary, the scanning of the entire code does not allow for the display of an error message until when the scan completes. This way, it limits the debugging process as the location of the bug becomes comparatively hard to trace.

Usability

As already mentioned, Python is among the few computer programming languages which use interpreters to translate source codes into machine codes. However, the use of compilers is optional in Python as interpreters are inbuilt and come within the package of Python. Therefore, Python and Ruby programming languages often write in Python language. Compilers are more useful in C, C++, and Java programming languages as they readily incorporate and translate source codes for different programming tools. This way, compilers are more valuable across all programming languages, including Python, despite the use of interpreters.

Python Compilers in Details

Truth be told, the use of Python compilers has been on the rise allowing developers to run programs from different programming tools. For example, a user may choose to write codes by using Java language, then translate it into Python or C/C++ to run an application. Besides, it can be used in different operating systems such as writing codes on Windows OS and running it on Linux or macOS without affecting the outcome. This is made possible as Python compilers are available in many different forms. Despite this, types of Python compilers have been categorized into online and offline.

Brython

This is one of the best Python compilers used in Python 3 today and is useful for developers to translate different codes. It is used globally and comes with features essential for translating codes into simple JavaScript codes. Besides, it can be further used through modifications to HTML5 and interfaces for DOM assignments. The functionalities of Brython are much faster in code translation, flexible, as well as secure when compared to other types such as CPython and Pypy.js.

Some of the features of Brython include the drag and drop functions for 3D navigations, compatibility with web browsers such as Firefox and mobile web browsers, and crucial in small and quick projects. As programming accompanies vary in programmable elements, Brython also includes different syntaxes such as comprehensions and generators. Besides, it also incorporates the properties of HTML5/CSS3 and utilizes BootStrap3 and LESS frameworks. Like most Python components, Brython also involves libraries that are used along with DOM and other modules.

CPython

Through referred to as an interpreter, CPython is one of the forms used as Python compiler written in C abs Python languages. Unlike other types of Python, CPython uses a Global Interpreter Lock, which executes Python bytecodes as single threads in each process of translation. It is, however, essential to run this process in a virtual machine as it is unsuitable go CPU complex algorithms. It is one of the best in the programming world, more so in Python due to its several standard libraries, which are C optimized. As an internally based

Python compiler, CPython uses the process of source code decoding, tokenizing, parsing, abstract syntax tree, and then compiling.

Tutorialspoint

Tutorialspoint is an online compiler, which is the most common and fastest tool to execute Python source codes. It is one of the free online Python compilers supporting both Python 2 and Python 3. It is used by millions of users around the globe, allowing the user to run codes within their computer browsers. More so, Tutorialspoint enables users to create and manage projects online, making it simple and easy to use as it offers high-performance levels, especially for analogous calculations. The key features of this compiler include color-coding capabilities, error display from source codes, and ability to download files and projects. This type of Python compiler is solely used for online code translation with therefore essential for web program running.

Nuitka

This is a source to source Python compiler primarily used to translate Python source codes or executables to C/C++. Even without using Python in the system, Nuitka is crucial in the development of standalone programs.

However, it only writes by use of Python language while using different libraries as well as extension modules often preferred by programmers. Like most Python compilers, Nuitka is available in different versions of Windows, macOS, Linux, and FreeBSD. It also accompanies a unique feature where it supports Anaconda crucial for the creation of programs used for data science and machine learning. Therefore, Nuitka is one of the few types of Python compiler which can operate outside Python while running in software for advancing other computer applications.

Repl.it

Another online Python compiler is the Repl.it. It is a capable compiler used to create, compile, and run codes. Like Tutorialspoint, it is used by millions around the world and supported by Python 2 and Python 3. Users who run code translation using Repl.it also have an advantage of sharing programs or source codes online with users globally. When running programs using this type of Python compiler, the programming section of the compiler often uses a virtual machine. The primary feature of this compiler is that it allows trainers to supply essential materials to all learners and enabling them to download the key components to practice.

WinPython

WinPython is primarily designed for Windows operating systems only and used as a modern Python compiler for the previous version of CPython. From the feedbacks of CPython users, they highlighted that the software had several bugs and errors which needed modifications. Therefore, it became the first release of WinPython to try and solve these problems and bringing out a more stable version. Unlike the previous CPython version, the WinPython compiler consists of numerous features with the addition of libraries and other vital elements. Some of the libraries present include NumPy and SciPy, essential for data science and machine learning projects.

This is an offline Python compiler that needs a download and installation process for the user to be able to use. However, the installer comes as a compressed file that requires unpacking then running the software. The integration is often straightforward and accompanies beneficial features. The limitation of this Python compiler is that it only translates Python to Java, and when downloading files, you have to choose which to download initially before running the installer.

Pythonanywhere

This is another online Python compiler and one of the unconventional used by a more significant number of users. Pythonanywhere is used globally and incorporates all web browsers and on any website. Already configured, this compiler does not require any download or installation but applied directly. Besides, it uses a maximum of 512mb of space while comprising numerous libraries, which include NumPy, BeautifulSoup, SciPy, and others preconfigured. It supports a version of Python 2.7 and selected Python 3. Available free of charge, it allows users to upload and download files readily with limited challenges when translating codes.

PyJS

PyJS are Python compilers that can be used both online and offline, depending on the source codes and the requirements of the user. That is, it can be used for code translation as well as run in web browsers while online. It is compatible with Python 3 versions and Python 2.7 and writes codes in Python language, which are translated to JavaScript executable codes online or in web browsers. It also includes an AJAX framework used as spacers for JS and DOM in different websites and browsers. When translating codes, PyJS uses a leveraged Python syntax tree, which facilitates the interaction between Python and JavaScript codes.

Supported by almost all operating systems, PyJS allows for the execution of codes in desktops using the PyJS module for web application source codes used as standalone. In other systems such as UNIX, they come with preinstalled versions having either JavaScript or Python codes though the same meaning under programming. Though some data types may change when running, the translation processes are often useful. Some of the standard features include direct web browser application, runtime support of instances of errors, and quick designing and development of programs because of code embedding in Python.

Hackerearth

Hackerearth is an online Python compiler allowing different users to translate and run codes live while viewing how each one proceeds. It often supports Python 2 and Python 3 and runs as a programming tool as different people can interact freely. As such, different people can engage on how to run codes in various computer programming languages while showing off their skills through Hackerearth. However, some may run isolated codes in sandboxed pathways while getting corrections in case of errors. Some of the features of this online Python compiler is that it allows an auto-complete option for completion of codes and highlighting basic syntaxes. Others include a timer, log ID displays, and usage of minimal memory spaces.

Shed Skin

Shed Skin primarily supports Python 2 versions, which range from Python 2.4, 2.5, and Python 2.6. This Python compiler solely deals with the translation of Python language into the C++ language. Shed Skin focuses on the variable conversion of single data types provided specific parameters but with limited features when compared to other Python compilers. Some of the features absent in Shed Skin include nested functions but accompany important standard libraries. The critical limitation of this type of compiler is that allows the translated codes to become optimized, therefore, may jeopardize the creation of programs.

Another significant limitation of Shed Skin is that it is unable to scale the higher number of codes, thus requiring the user to analyze it manually. For example, when the system recognizes unsupported features or modules during the translation process, it would need you to go ahead and remove IG manually by supplying the system with plan codes for ease of identification. As such, most developers have term it an experimental compiler though it provides exceptional outcomes. The results are often standalone programs and extension modules used in significant Python programs for the development of productive applications.

JDoodle

When writing codes online, there are instances where short lines of codes may occur, hence the need for efficient software to run it effectively. JDoodle is an online Python compiler that delivers adequate results, especially in running, storing, and sharing created programs online. It is a free online Python compiler supporting Python 2 and Python 3 versions. With different Python standard libraries available online, JDoodle utilizes entire libraries to ensure the delivery of exceptional outcomes. When you run your programs online using JDoodle, the results often appear on the window, allowing you to share codes. Again, the edit, run, and share options are readily integrated within the software for ease of access by users.

Ideone

This is one of Python tools that can be used as both a compiler and debugger but solely used as online software. The compilations and running of codes are normally done in over 50 programming languages. Like most online Python compilers, Ideone supports Python 2 and Python 3 versions, which accompany the Sphere Engine Technology to allow the execution of programs securely and remotely. As such, users can either run programs privately or publicly. Ideone features include error message display, color coding, and learning abilities, among others. The Sphere Engine is one of the features which separate this online compiler from the rest. The primary benefit of this compiler is that it allows for content management and configuration of programming modules within Python.

Other Benefits of Using Python Compilers

Improved Performance

Everyone loves efficiency, especially when running programs in different machines or under a set of parameters. When using compilers, the level of performance improvement is likely to be observed though it primarily depends on the program. However, using Python compilers and interpreters have proven to increase the performance of program execution, therefore, yielding a more productive outcome.

Reduced Lagging

When compared to interpreters on source code translation, Python compilers are much quicker. This is because the program has to be only translated at once with much higher response time. Therefore, there are minimal chances of system loads, which often results in lagging, when running more programs.

Source Code Protection

When you have your set codes and ready to translate, your primary goal is to ensure you keep your programs and algorithms secure. That is, you tend to ensure that it is not changed in any way to affect the end results. However, compilers are often crucial as it helps in source code and program protection as computers only translate codes after a complete and successful scan.

Increased Productivity

Compliers are often crucial in the production of source listing and messages, which help in Python maintenance. That is, you can quickly identify errors through messages displays and run your debugger to solve the problem. As such, you can make corrections and run programs with minimal mistakes, hence improving your productivity and quality of work.

Allowance for Portability

Python allows programs to be translated in different operating systems as well as in other computer programming languages. This way, programs can be written at one machine and transferred to another computer, which uses a different computer language and runs efficiently. Henceforth, compilers allow portability between different programming languages.

Chapter 5: Python Coding and Python Variables

Python is one of the most common programming languages used in the web development sector today. It is a general-purpose, high-level, interpreted programming language. It was created by Guido van Rossum and was initially released in the early 1990s. Python programming language is designed in a way that it focuses on code readability through the significant whitespace. Python programming uses an object-oriented and language constructs that focus on helping programmers write logical and clear codes. Programmers can write code for both small and large-scale projects.

Python programming language is typed dynamically and garbage-collected. It offers support for multiple paradigms in programming. Such models include functional, procedural, and object-oriented programming. Python language is commonly defined as a battery-included programming language. It is because of its extensive standard library.

The conception of Python programming language was a succession to the ABC language. The release of Python 2.0 was made in 2000. It had features such as list comprehensions and garbage collection systems. These systems were able to collect reference cycles. In 2008, Python 3.0 was released. It was a primary revision of the programming language that is not fully backward-compatible. Python 2.0 code has to be modified for it to run on Python 3. There was an extension on the support for Python 2.7 to 2020 due to increased concerns on the amount of code that could be written on Python 2.0. The Python programming language developer, van Rossum was entirely responsible for the project. However, in July 2018, he shared out his roles and currently works as a member of a steering council chaired by five members.

The Python 2.7x language is set to be released by 1st January 2020. The Python programmers working as volunteers on the project will not continue fixing security conditions or improving the programming language in any other way after that date. Towards the end-of-life, only Python 3.5x will be supported. There are numerous Python interpreters available for almost all operating systems. There is a global group of programmers that are responsible for the development and maintenance of CPython is an open-source reference implementation.

The Python Software Foundation is a non-profit organization that focuses on the management and direction for the resources for CPython and Python development.

Features and Philosophy

Python is considered as a multi-paradigm programming language. Structured and object-oriented programming are wholly supported by Python. Additionally, some of the features of the Python programming language support aspect-oriented and functional programming. These are inclusive of meta-objects and metaprogramming. Other programming paradigms are supported through extensions such as logic and design by contract programming.

Python makes use of dynamic typing combined with reference counting and garbage collectors that are cycle-detecting. They work in this way for the efficient management of memory. Python is also characterized by dynamic name resolution, also known as late binding. The name resolution helps in binding variable names and methods during the execution of programs. Python programming language design also allows for the support of functional programming within the Lisp tradition. It has three functions, namely filter, map, and reduce. It also has dictionaries, generator expressions, sets, and list comprehensions. The standard library contains two modules known as functools and itertools that help in the implementation of functional tools that are borrowed from Standard ML and Haskell.

The core philosophy of the Python programming language is summarized in The Zen of Python document. It contains some aphorisms like explicit is way better than implicit, readability counts, the complex is much better than complicated, simple is better than complex, and beautiful is way better than ugly. Instead of having every of its functionality centrally built on it, Python programming language was designed in a way that it is highly extensible. Its compact modularity has made it gain popularity. It is used as a way of adding programmable interfaces to already existing applications. Van Rossum was frustrated with the ABC programming language, and therefore, focused on coming up with a programming language that had a smaller central language but with a substantial standard library. He also visioned coming up with a programming language that would be highly extensible.

The main aim of Python is simplicity, less-cluttered grammar and syntax as well as allowing web developers to choose their coding methodologies. Python programming language embraces the fact that there should be one, and most preferably, only one obvious way to do something. This design philosophy has guided Python programmers until now. Python developers are also governed by the philosophy that in the Python culture, describing something as clever is never considered as a compliment.

Developers who are working on Python programming language focus on avoiding premature optimizations they often reject spots on the non-critical areas of the reference on CPython implementation that would increase speed while compromising clarity. There are alternatives made available for Python programmers because speed is critical. One of the vital goals of Python developers is ensuring that it is fun to use. The name of the programming language practically reflects the fun in it. The approaches used in reference materials and tutorials are occasionally very playful.

One of the common analogies used in the programming language community is Pythonic. The term has broad meanings concerning program style. Referring to code as Pythonic means it is using Python idioms appropriately, it is natural, and has a good fluency in the programming language. It also means that it is conforming to the minimalist philosophy in Python, readability, and emphasis. On the other hand, unPythonic code is challenging to read and understand. Pythonistas are the admirers and users of Python. The term is primarily given to people who are more skilled and knowledgeable with the Python programming language.

Syntax and Semantics

The main focus of Python programming language is making code easier to read and understand. It uses virtually uncluttered formatting where English keywords are used instead of punctuations. Python does not make use of curly brackets like in other programming languages. The English keywords are used in delimiting blocks. Python has minimal syntactic exceptions and unique cases than Pascal or C.

Indentation

Whitespace indentation is mainly used in delimiting blocks. It is used instead of keywords or curly brackets. Increasing indentation comes after some particular statements, whereas decreasing indentation shows an end of the current blocks. The visual structures of the program act as representations of the semantic structures of the programs. The feature is at times referred to as the off-side rule. Enforcement of indentations in Python programming makes its code look more neat and clean. The uncluttered code in Python makes programs look alike and consistent.

Statements and Control Flow

There are numerous statements used in the Python programming language. They include some of the following.

- The assignment statement. The operations of this statement differ from the traditional imperative programming languages. The underlying mechanism calls for the illumination of multiple characteristics of the programming language.

- The "if" statement. It is used in the conditional execution of code blocks. It is used together with "else" and "elif".

- The "for" statement. It works as iterations over some iterable objects. It captures every element and places them on local variables where the attached blocks use them.

- The "while" statement. The statement is used in the execution of code blocks anytime the condition is real.

- The "raise" statement. It is used when raising particular exceptions or re-raising caught exceptions.

- The "class' statement. It is used in the execution of code blocks and attaching their local namespace to classes. This connection is later used in object-oriented programming.

- The 'def" statement. This statement is used in the definition of functions or methods.

- The "pass" statement. It works as the NOP. The statement is practically needed when creating empty blocks of code.

- The "import" statement. The statement is used when importing modules whose variables and functions are applicable in a currently running program. There are multiple ways through which the "import" statement can be used in Python programming.

- The "yield" statement. It is used in returning values from a generator function.

First-class continuations and tail-call optimizations are not supported by Python, and there is no possibility of the two being supported.

Expressions

Some of the expressions used in Python are similar to most programming languages such as Java and C.

- Subtraction, multiplication, and addition are used similarly. The behavior of division, however, differs quite much. Two types of division are used in Python programming. These include the floor division, also referred to as the integer division, and the floating-point division. The "* *" operators were later added to Python for exponentiation.

- The new '@" infix operator introduction was made from Python 3.5. The main intention was using it in libraries, including NumPy for multiplication of the matrix.

- The "= = "is used for making comparisons between values vs Java. It is used in comparing numeric through objects and values by references.

- A word such as "and", "not", and "or" are used by Python for its Boolean operators instead of symbolic "& &" that are used in C and Java.

- The 'list comprehension' is a form of expression used in Python.

Python Variables

Python variables are reserved memory locations where values are stored. Variables in Python programs are responsible for giving data to the computer for the purposes of the processing. Each value in Python holds a data type. Various data types in Python include Strings, Tuple, Numbers, List, and Dictionary. The variables are easily declared through any name or alphabets like ABC.

Python variables can also be described as buckets or envelopes where information is referenced and maintained. Similar to other programming languages, Python programming uses the variables to store useful information. Whenever a Python variable is created, it means that some space has been reserved in the memory.

Depending on the data type of different variables, interpreters work on allocating memory and deciding what should be stored in the reserved memory space. Therefore, through assigning of varied data types to variables, a programmer can easily store characters, decimals, and integers in the Python variables.

Assigning Values to Variables

Python variables do not require explicit declarations for memory space to be reserved. There is an automatic declaration that occurs anytime a value is assigned to a variable. The equal sign is used when assigning values to Python variables. The operand on the left side of the equal sign operator is considered as the name of the particular Python variable. The operand on the right side of the equal sign operator is referred to as the value that is stored within the variable.

Multiple Assignment

Python programming makes it possible for a programmer to assign single values to multiple variables concurrently. For instance:

```
a=b-c-1
```

In the above case, the integer object has been created with 1 as the value. All three variables have been assigned to the same memory space. Multiple objects can also be assigned to several variables simultaneously. For instance:

```
a,b,c=1,2 "Sean"
```

In the above case, two integer objects have values 1 and 2 and have been assigned to two variables that are a and b. A single string object has the value Sean has been assigned to the c variable. The above examples illustrate how multiple assignments are done in Python programming.

Standard Data Types

The data that is stored within the memory can occur in various types. For instance, an individual's age can be stored in number values, whereas their address can be stored in alphanumeric characters. Python programming language offers different data types used in the definition of operations that are possible on them. They also help in defining storage methods that are supported by each of them. The five standard data types in Python include string, tuple, dictionary, and numbers.

Python number data types are used for the storage of numeric values. When values are assigned to the number of data types, number objects are formed. The "del" statement can be used when deleting the references to particular numbers. A programmer can delete one or multiple objects through the use of the "del" statement.

Python String data types are recognized as an attached set of characters that are represented within the quotation marks. Python programming offers support for both single and double-quotes. A slice operator can be used when taking subsets of the strings.

Python List data types are considered to be the most versatile compound data types in Python. Python lists consist of multiple items that are separated by commas and are enclosed inside square brackets. There are instances where Python lists are similar to the C arrays. However, they differ in that the items present on Python lists can be from varying data types. Values that are stored within a list can be accessed through the use of slice operators together with indexes starting from 0 at the start of the list.

Python Tuples data types occur as sequences similar to the Python list data type. Python tuples consist of the number of values that are separated by the use of commas. Tuples are, however, enclosed inside parentheses. One main difference between lists and tuples is that the elements on lists can vary and their size can be changed. The aspects of tuples, on the other hand, cannot be changed or updated. They are referred to as read-only lists.

Python Dictionary data types occur in the form of hash table types. They perform their roles as associative hashes or arrays found on Perl. They all consist of pairs of key-values. Python dictionaries are enclosed within curly brackets. The square brackets are, on the other hand, used when assigning and accessing the values encompassed in the dictionaries' values. There is no concept of order found in elements on Python dictionaries. The elements in these dictionaries are typically unordered.

Data Type Conversion

There are several times when programmers require to perform conversions among built-in data types. Performing conversions between Python data types requires a programmer to use the type name in place of a function. Various built-in functions are used in the conversion of one data type to another. The functions perform their roles by returning new objects to represent the values that have been converted. The float (x) is used when converting x to floating-point numbers, str(x) is used when converting object x strings representations, and eva(str) is used in evaluating strings and returning objects.

Python Variables can be easily declared by the use of any name or alphabet. Below is an example of how to declare and use a Python variable.

In this case, we shall declare variable "d" and print it.

a=100

print a

It is possible for programmers to re-declare variables once they have been declared.

Concatenate Variables

Python programming requires the number to be declared as strings when concatenating variables. This is unlike in other programming languages such as Java where numbers are concatenated without necessarily declaring them as strings.

Local and Global Variables

There are several instances where Python programmers require to use a similar variable for the entire module or program. This means that they have first to declare the variable as a global one. In cases where they want to use a particular function in a precise method or function, they will use local variables. There are several differences between local and global variables. The differences can be identified in the program below.

1. Variable: y" is global in scope and assigned the value 202 that is printed in the output.

2. Variable y is once more declared in function and takes on the local scope. It can be assigned the value "I am trying to understand Python." The value is also printed as output. The variable

becomes different from the global variable "y' initially defined.

3. After the function role is over, there is a destruction of the local variable y. When the value of 'y" is printed again, it displays the global value variable as y=202.

Through the use of the global keyword, a programmer can easily access the global variable within a function.

Deleting a Variable

When deleting variables, programmers should use the command "del", together with the variable name. Once a variable is deleted, printing it is not possible because the variable has already been eliminated.

Declaring local variables in Python is more efficient when a programmer wants to apply it in current functions. Declaring local variables, on the other hand, is useful when a similar variable is being used for an entire module.

Variable Names

Python variables can be assigned short names such as y and z or descriptive names such as total-volume, age, and home address. Several rules guide Python variables. They include the following.

- The Python variable name should start with an underscore character or a letter.
- The Python variable name must not start with a number or a numeric figure.
- The Python variable name should only contain characters that are alphanumeric and underscores. They are, for instance, a-z and 0-9.
- Python variable names are case-sensitive. For example, Age, age, and AGE are different Python variables. This means that a slight mistake in typing can result in errors in the entire module or program. It can also lead to misinterpretation of the modules. Programmers need to be very careful when coding to avoid such errors.

Advantages of Python Programming Language

Python programming language has gone through significant diversifications for it to be applied in software and web development sectors such as gaming. Such diversification has given the language high popularity as compared to other languages that are used in programming. Some of the advantages of Python programming language include:

- **Extensive support libraries.** Python provides maximum standard libraries. These libraries consist of areas such as web service tools, string operations, operating system protocols and interfaces, web service, and the Internet.

- **Python programming language has some integration features.** Python programming supports the integration of Enterprise Application. This integration makes it easier for a programmer to come up with Web services by entreating COBRA or COM. Python has incredible capabilities to control programs through C++, C, and Java. Python can as well apply similar byte codes to run on all modernized operating systems.

- **Python allows for improved productivity of the programmer.** Python language offers incredible extensive support libraries. It also provides some neat object-oriented designs. A combination of the two helps in enhancing the productivity of the programmer. With the strong process through which

Python integrates its features, it helps in increasing the speed of many applications. An improved speed means improved productivity of applications.

From the above advantages, it is essential to also note that most companies prefer hiring programmers who are well conversant with the Python language. The main reason for this is its speed and efficiency. It is, therefore, one of the vital things one should consider learning in their programming course.

Chapter 6: Best Ways to Learn Python Programming

Firstly, Python is an object-oriented programming language for developing both desktop and web applications and complex scientific and numeric applications. It helps the programmer to write clear, logical code for small and larger-scale projects. Python is garbage collected and dynamically typed. It supports programming paradigms such as object-oriented, procedural, and functional programming. The programming language was conceived in 1980s to succeed the ABC language. In 2000, Python 2.0 was released which introduced features like a garbage collection system and list comprehensions that can collect reference cycles. In 2008, Python 3.0 was released with a major revision of the language that cannot be completely down warded.

On January 1, 2020, Python 2.7.x was 'sunsetting' and the volunteer team was not fixing security issues. They might not be in apposition to advance it after the date. With the end-of-sale of Python 2.7.x, only Python 3.5.x will be given the support. Many operation systems are supported by Python interpreters. CPython is developed and maintained by a global community of programmers as an open-source of the reference implementation. Python and CPython development are managed and directed by a Python software foundation which is a non-profit making organization.

In the 1980s, Guido van Rossum, in Netherlands at Centrum Wiskunde and Informatica, came up with Python. This was to succeed the ABC language which was inspired by SETL. Van Rossum remained as a Python lead developer until 12th July 2018 when he announced his retirement from the responsibilities of Pythons. As the project's chief decision-maker, he was named *benevolent Dictator of Life* by the Python community. Brett Connon, Carol Willing, Barry Warsaw, and Nick Coghlan were elected in January 2019 as the Python core developers to lead the project. On 16 October 2000, Python 2.0 was released with new features for support of Unicode and cycle-detecting garbage collector. On 3rd December 2008, Python 3 was released with a major revision of the language backward-compatible. The release of Python 3 included the 2 to 3 utility that partially releases Python 2 code to Python 3 translation. The end-of-life date of Python 2.7 begun in 2015, then postponed to 2020 because Python 3 cannot be easily forward-ported.

Features and Philosophy

Python programming features support the aspect-oriented metaprogramming and metaobjects to fully support this structured and object-oriented programming. Logic programming and design contracts via extensions support many paradigms.

In the Lisp tradition, Python's design gives support for functional programming. This has filter, reduced functions and map listing comprehensions, dictionaries, generator expressions, and sets. The stand library has itertools and functools modules that plan the functional tools borrowed from standard ML and Haskell.

The Zen of Python (PEP 20) summarizes the language's core philosophy that includes aphorism such as readability counts

- Ugly is worse than beautiful
- Implicit is worse than explicit
- Simple is better than hard
- Complicated is worse than complex

Python is designed in a highly extensible manner instead of having its core built on its functionality. While giving the developer an option of their coding methodology, Python strives to be grammar-free, less-cluttered syntax, and simpler. The extension module that is written in language C, used by PyPy, can be moved time-critical by Python programmer. The Python script is translated to C and made direct C-level API by the Cython.

Its essential goal is to keep Python's developers to enjoy its use. Pythonic is a common neologism in the Python community that has a large number of meanings related to program style. When the code uses Python idioms, it is said to be *Pythonic* and that it complies with Python's minimalist emphasis and philosophy on readability. The code is said to be *unPythonic* when it has challenges in understanding or be read like a rough transcription, while the *Pythoniastas* are persons that are considered to be knowledgeable and experienced.

Python is visually uncluttered and frequently uses English keywords in places where other languages use punctuation, thus it is an easily readable language. In this programming method, semicolons statements are optional, and it does not use curly brackets to set blocks. Unlike Pascal or C, it has fewer special cases and syntactic exceptions.

Indentation

Rather than curly brackets to delimit blocks, Python programming uses white space indentation. A decrease in indentation shows the end of the current blocks while the increase comes after a particular statement. The off-side rule is a feature that shows the program's visual structure accurately. This indentation makes Python's programming look clean and neat and results in a consistent and similar look at the program.

Statement and control flow

The equals (=) is an assignment statement in Python programming. Other features of the language are, in many ways illuminated, in the fundamental mechanism that operates differently compared to the traditional imperative languages of programming.

Typing

Python programming language allows its users to define their typing method by classifying them into their own classes. New instances of classes are built by naming the class EggClass or SpamClass. The classes are instances of the metaclass that lead to reflection and metaprogramming. Classes are also prototypes that used to create objects.

Old-style and new-style are the two kinds of classes that were there before version 3.0. The difference between the two classes is whether the class object is inherited directly or indirectly while the similarity is that both styles have a similar syntax of styles. The version of Python 2 from Python 2.2 uses both kinds of classes. Compile-time type checking is supported by an optional experimental static type checker.

Tips to Learn Python for a Beginner

Firstly, for anyone to learn the programming language, they must understand how to learn because this is the most critical skill in computer programming. Below is the journey to becoming a Python programmer.

Make It Stick

This is enhanced by the consistency in the willingness to learn. Coding every day is one commitment to learning the new language. One develops muscle memory once they commit to coding every day. This can be enhanced by beginning with as small as 25 minutes each day.

Besides that, write it out to make it stick. As a new programmer, you should take notes for reference. The notes are helpful for those aiming to become a full-time programmer because many interviews involve writing of the codes. Writing helps to plan one's code when they start working with small programs and projects. If you write out the function and class that you need as well as the way they interact, you can save a lot of time.

Go interactive. Interactive Python shell is the best learning tool whether it is the first time one is learning about Python structures and data, or they are debugging an application. To allow the use of a Python shell, one should make sure they have installed Python on her computer. Open your terminal to run Python or Python3 to activate Python shell.

Take breaks. During the learning sessions, always ensure you can absorb the language of programming by stepping away for a while. To have effective study sessions, it is critical to take some short breaks, especially if a lot of information is new. When you hit a bug while debugging, and you do not know how you hit it, take a break before going back to the computer to allow the absorption of knowledge. Following the rules of language and logic allow coding to run smoothly without breaking.

Become a bug bounty hunter to allow the Python language to stick. When writing complex programs, one may find themselves hitting the bug in coding. One can embrace this by allowing themselves to imagine themselves as a bug bounty hunter. During the session of debugging, it is advisable to have a methodology bring things back to normal. You may insert import pdb; pdb.set_trace() in your script and run it once you notice where things may be breaking down. Here, you will be dropped into interactive mode by the Python debugger which can learn a command-line Python –m pdb <my_file.py>.

Make It Collaborative. Collaboration allows one to expedite their learning once the programming language starts to stick. This is enhanced by the learner surrounding himself with other people who are learning. When people work together, coding works best, because it is a solitary activity. When you surround yourself with people who are learning Python, you can easily share your tips and also learn from them.

Teach. The best way of learning Python is to teach it to other people who may be interested in the same. There are several ways of teaching Python which includes talking to you at the computer, one can record a video of something they learned, whiteboard with Python lovers, and explaining new concept into a blog. This will facilitate understanding of the programming language.

Pair program. This is collaborative because two programmers in a workstation merge to complete the task. The two change between being a 'driver' and the 'navigator'. Here, the 'navigator' solves the problem as he assesses the code as it is written by the 'driver'. The two switches severally to gain the benefit of both sides. The developer can benefit by getting a chance to review the code and to see how the other person thinks about the code. This helps one to have problem-solving skills ones they return to coding by themselves.

Make Something. Most Python developers encourage one to learn Python by doing something. For a starter, it is advisable if they have basic data to try to start building a small project. Here, how you build a project is what is important rather than what you build. This is because the journey of creating using Python is what teaches you the concept of your project. A beginner can try a simple calculator app or a dice roll simulator. When the beginner finds difficulties in projects of Python language, you should watch blogs of other developers to instill the right strategy of coming up with the Python project

Best Steps to Learning Python

Figure out what motivates you to learn Python

This is because learning Python will not be easy, therefore, one needs to have a motivation to start the journey. Ensure you have reasons for studying this programming language so that you can find a reason for not giving up when the journey gets tough. Here you have to set a final goal so that you can use it as a motivation when you lose focus. Pick an area of interest among mobile apps, games, robots, data science, and scripts to automate your work that you are willing to stick with. One should choose an area that you have an interest in.

Learn Basic Syntax

Before one dive deeper into any chosen area, they must learn basic Python syntax. Learn basics through the following ways:

- Codeacademy does a good job when one is learning the basics because it builds on itself well

- Learn the programming language the hard way through a book that teaches Python concepts right from the first concept.

- Dataquest makes learning the Python language easier. This is because Dataquest in the context of learning data science teaches Python syntax. For instance, while analyzing weather you will learn about for loops.

- Learning through Python tutorials that are of the main Python site.

Make Structured Projects

When one has learned the basic syntax, they can start their projects. This is because projects are a better way to learn when one gets a chance to apply the learned knowledge. In applying your knowledge through the project, one will be in a position to build a portfolio for a potential employer, one can learn new things, and the projects will display one's capability in Python programming. Resources of Python programming have structured projects that build interesting things in the area that one is concentrating in and prevent one from getting stuck. Also, data science courses help one to apply their new skills when one is learning Python of data science.

Structured projects that one can venture into include:

Data Science

- Dataquest asks one to write real code to analyze world data because each code ends with a guided project.

- Python data analysis helps one to learn some skills they need for building data science projects.

- Scikit-learn documentation, the main machine learning library, has some great tutorials and documentation that one can use to work through them to know how it feels and how the Python language is used.

- CS109 is a Harvard class that teaches data science of Python, and it has projects and materials online that one can use while enrolling in the language.

Building Mobile Apps

Kivy_guide in Python allows you to make mobile apps because they contain a guide on how to get started with the project.

Websites

- Flask tutorial in Python is a popular web framework because it is an introductory tutorial.

- Bottle tutorial is a web framework that shows how to get started in Python language.

- How to Tango with Django is a complex framework website in this programming language that has a guide to using Django.

Games

- Codeacademy is used to make a couple of simple games through its interactive lessons.

- Pygame tutorials are popular for making games in Python library

- Making _games with Pygame is a book in Python programming that teaches how to make games.

- Invent your computer with Python is a book in this programming language that teaches you to learn how to make games.

Hardware/Robots/ Sensors

- Using Python with Arduino teaches one to know how to use Python by connecting to Arduino.

- Learning Python with Raspberry Pi gives one a place to start in Python and a Raspberry Pi while building a hardware project.

- Learning robotics using Python helps one to learn how you can build a robot in Python language.

- Raspberry Pi Cookbook helps one to build robots using the Python language and Rasberry.

Scripts to Automate Work

Automate the boring stuff with Python is a book that teaches one to automate with the Python language.

Work on the Project on Your Own

In this fourth way to learn Python, you should come up with a unique project. This will help you to know whether you have learned. While coming up with your project, you will have a chance to learn new concepts while consulting different sources to come up with a legit project. Debugging errors and problems with one's programs should not be a problem before one thinks of coming up with their projects. The sources below will help you through:

- StackOverflow is a site where people discuss issues of programming because it is a community with questions and answers. In this site, a person can find all the questions of Python, and their answers and search always reveal when someone else has asked the same question before.

- Google is a tool that is commonly used by every experienced developer.

- Python's official documentation in Python programming is a good place to find reference material for the language.

Once you are familiar with how to deal with debugging issues, it will be easier for you to work freely on your project. One should ensure they work on the areas of their interests to have the motivation and to avoid getting stuck. Below are some of the tips for finding interesting projects:

- Ensure you add more functionality and extend the projects that you were working on before.

- Find people who are working on projects of Python programming by going to the areas of their meetups.

- Contribute to an open-source package.

- Volunteer in any local nonprofits' developers.

- Go to Github to find other people who have projects and try to extend or adapt to them

- Go through other peoples' blogs and posts to find interesting ideas for their projects.

- Find and build tools for Python that can make your life easier.

To gain confidence, one is advised to begin with things that are simple, and start a small project that you can finish than a huge one that will not be finished. Also, get motivation by working with other developers so that you can get challenged. Below are some of the good project ideas in each area to help one choose.

Data Science

- ➤ An algorithm that forecasts weather

- ➤ A tool that forecasts stock market

- ➤ A map that reflects election data by state

- ➤ An algorithm that simply summarizes new articles

- ➤ Mobile apps

- ➤ An app that emits weather notifications

- ➤ An app that follows how you walk every day

- ➤ A chat app that is of real-time location

Websites

- ➤ A website that assists you in organizing weekly meals

- ➤ A site that permits users to assess video games

- ➤ A platform for note-taking

Games

- ➤ A game that players use to resolve puzzles with written code

- ➤ A mobile game that captures territory in a location

Robots/ Sensors/Hardware

- ➤ Create a robot that is self-driving and detects obstacles

- ➤ Create a smarter alarm clock

- ➤ Build temperature, moisture, and CO2 sensors to monitor one's house.

- ➤ Scripts to automate your work

- ➤ A script that reminds one to stand up every hour.

- ➤ A script that automates data entry

Keep Working on Progressively Harder Projects

When one gets comfortable with their projects, it means they can handle harder ones and thus they are encouraged to try. Below are some of the ideas for increasing the project's complexity while you are learning.

> Try to teach your project to other people. This will enable the whole idea to sink in your mind.

> Ensure you know whether your tool can work and handle other data including more traffic.

> Ensure your program can run faster

> Ensure you know how to commercialize what you have come up with

Python evolves every now and then, therefore, you need to keep working and learning the projects. When one keeps doing this, you will be on the right track of becoming a good developer in this programming language. One should keep exploring things in this program to avoid boredom when specializing in only what interests you. When one gets the right motivation in learning the language, you can have a high-level proficiency.

Chapter 7: Python Debugging

Like most computer programming languages, Python utilizes debugging processes for the benefit of providing exceptional computing programs. The software enables you to run applications within the specified debugger set with different breakpoints. Similarly, interactive source code is provided to a Python program for the benefit of supporting under program controls. Other actions of a debugger in Python are testing of units and integration, analysis of log files and log flows as well as system-level monitoring.

Running a program within the debugger comprises several tools working depending on a given command line and IDE systems. For instance, the development of more sophisticated computer programs has significantly contributed to the expansion of debugging tools. The tools accompany various methods of detecting Python programming abnormalities, evaluation of its impacts, and plan updates and patches to correct emerging problems. In some cases, debugging tools may improve programmers in the development of new programs by eliminating code and Unicode faults.

Debugging

Debugging is the technique used in detecting and providing solutions to either defects or problems within a specific computer program. The term 'debugging' was first accredited to Admiral Grace Hopper while working at Harvard University on Mark II computers in the 1940s. She discovered several months between relays, thereby hindering computer operations and named them 'debugging' in the system. Despite the term previously used by Thomas Edison in 1878, debugging began becoming popular in the early 1950s with programmers adopting its use in referring to computer programs.

By the 1960s, debugging gained popularity between computer users and the most common term mentioned to described solutions to major computing problems. With the world becoming more digitalized with challenging programs, debugging has covered a significant scope. Henceforth, eliminating words like computer errors, bugs, and defects to a more neutral one such as computer anomaly and discrepancy. However, the neutral terms are also under impact assessment to determine if their definition of computing problems provides a cost-effective manner to the system or more changes be made. The assessment tries to create a more practical term to define computer problems while retaining the meaning but preventing end-users from denying the acceptability of faults.

Anti-Debugging

Anti-debugging is the opposite of debugging and encompasses the implementation of different techniques to prevent debugging processes or reverse engineering in computer codes. The process is primarily used by developers, for example, in copy-protection schemes as well as malware to identify and prevent debugging. Anti-debugging is, therefore, the complete opposite of debugger tools which include prevention of detection and removal of errors that occasionally appear during Python programming. Some of the conventional techniques used are:

- API-based
- Exception-based
- Modified code
- Determining and penalizing debugger
- Hardware-and register-based
- Timing and latency

Concepts of Python Debugging

Current Line

The current line is a notion where a computer only has to do only one thing at any given time, especially when creating programs. The flow of codes typically is controlled from one point to another with activities only running on the current line to the next below the screen. In Python programming, the current path can only be changed with functions such as loops, IF statements, and calls among others. It is also not a must to begin programming from the first line, but you can use breakpoints to decide where to start and where to avoid.

Breakpoints

When you are running programs in Python package, the codes will usually begin writing from the first line and run continuously until when there is a success or error. However, bugs may occur either in a specific function or a section of the program, but the error codes may not have been used during input. The error may persist until during the start of the program that you notice the problem. At this point, breakpoints become useful as they readily stop these events. Breakpoints alter debuggers where the problem is and immediately halts program execution and make necessary corrections.

This concept, therefore, enables you to create excellent Python programming languages within a short time.

Stepping

Stepping is another concept which operates with debugging tools in making programs more efficient. Python program stepping is the act of jumping through codes to determine if program lines with defects as well as any other mistakes which need attention before execution. Stepping in different codes occurs as step-ins, step over, and step out. Step in entails the completion of the next line filled with systems making the user skip into codes and debug the intended one. Step over refers to a developer moving to the following line in the existing function and debug with a new code before running the program. Step out command refers to skipping to the last line of the program and making completions of the codes before executing the plan.

Continuous Program Execution

There are some cases where Python programming may result in continuing program execution by the computer itself. The continue command gives your computer the control of resuming code input until the end unless there exists another breakpoint. The resume button may vary depending on the computer operating systems or the

119

types of language programming packages. However, there exist several similarities between them making Python debugging more adaptable to different end-users and developers.

Existing Debugging Tool

The primary purpose of acquiring a debugger tool is to identify and eliminate problems. After utilizing debugger functionalities of detecting an error or problem within the program or codes, correction of the problem follows. The sequence will include fixing of the failure by rewriting the characters, stopping debugging processes, insert a breakpoint on the fixed-line, and launch another debugger tool. Similar, the procedure may vary depending on the OS and the other packages other than Python.

Function Verification

When writing codes into the program, it is vital to keep track of the state of each code, especially on calculations and variables. Similarly, the growth of functions may stake up, leading to creating a function calling technique to understand how each task affects the next one. Likewise, it is recommended entering the nested codes first when it comes to stepping in to develop a sequential approach of executing the right codes first.

Understanding Debugging and Python Coding

Before venturing more in-depth into the connection between the program and debugging associated, there exist different ways of how the application performs behaves. One of the significant components of debugging is that it runs codes within your program one at a time and enables you to see the process of data execution. They act as instant replays of what has occurred in the Python program with a step-by-step tutorial hence seeing the semantic errors occurred.

When the code is being executed, your computer may provide a limited view of what is happening; hence, debuggers make it possible for you to see them. As such, the Python program should behave like slow motion graphics while identifying the errors or bugs present within the codes. As such, the debugger enables you to determine the following:

- The flow of codes in the program

- The techniques used to create variables

- Specific data contained in each variable within the program

- The addition, modification, and elimination of functions

- Any other types of calculations performed

- Code looping

- How the ID and ELSE statements have been entered

Debugger Commands

With debugging being a common feature in the programming language, there exist several commands used when maneuvering between various operations. The basic controls are the most essential for beginners and may include an abbreviation of one or more letters. A blank space must separate the command while others are enclosed in brackets. However, the syntax command does not allow for the square brackets to be written but separated alternatively by a vertical bar. In Python programs, statements are rarely recognized by debugger commands executed within the parameters of the program.

To inspect Python statements against errors and other related faults, prefixes are added with an exclamation mark, henceforth, making it possible to make changes on variables as well as function calls. Several commands may also be inserted in the same line but separated by

';;' with inputs spaced separately from other codes. As such, debugging is said to work with aliases, which allows for adaptability between words in the same context. Besides, aliases enhance the need for reading files in the directory with faults but seen as correct with the use of the debugger prompt.

Chapter 8: Top Python Libraries

Multi-dimensional object-oriented programming languages have libraries. A Python library is a collection of methods and functions that permits the programmer to perform many actions without writing your code. A method explains the behavior of the objects that get derived from a class. Functions are statements that perform inputs processes for them to produce outputs. A function must get called for it to run. Top Python libraries include:

Fire

This is a library that has an open-source that automatically generates command-line interfaces (CLIs) with a single line of code. It executes your command hence the name fire. It runs by calling the fire method than passing it to what you wanted to turn into a CLI. It may be a class, dictionary, an object or a function.

Here are some of the methods that can be used to call the fire command.

Fire.Fire() that gets called at the end of the program. It will show the full contents of the application to the command line.

Fire.Fire(object) works on objects which get derived from a class. It exposes various commands.

Fire.Fire(class) performs tasks in classes. They are templates that get used to create objects. It also exposes multiple commands.

Fire.Fire(<dict>) This one carefully shows functions to the command line.

Luminoth

It is an open-source tool kit for vision in computers and object detection. Python 2.7 and 3.4 to 3.6 get supported by luminoth. It is built using Sonnet and TensorFlow. TensorFlow is a platform for machine learning (ML) which is open-source. It contains community resources, ecosystem tools, and libraries that allow developers to deploy and build ML-powered applications and researchers push the state-of-art- in ML. Sonnet is a library built to give pure abstractions for research. It gets built on top of TensorFlow2.

TensorFlow must be installed for one to use luminoth. The command-line interface that one can use is only one, Lumi - -help or Lumi <subcommand>--help. This demonstrates a list of available options.

Theano

It is a Python library that permits you to evaluate, define, and optimize mathematical expressions involving multi-dimensional arrays. It is developed by a machine learning group that is why it is a compiler for mathematical expressions. The following are features for Theano:

- Dynamic C code generation that allows faster evaluation of expressions.
- It has efficient symbolic differentiation which does derivatives for functions that has one or many inputs.
- Tight integration with NumPy utilizes numpy.ndarray in Theano-compiled functions.
- It allows transparent utilization of a GPU which carries out data-intensive computations much faster than on a CPU.
- Speed and stability optimizations that get the appropriate answer for log(1+x) when x is tiny.
- Extensive unit-testing and self-verification detects hence diagnosing many types of errors.

Request

It is an HTTP library which is Apache2 licensed and written in Python. It is created to be utilized by humans to interact with the programming language. Humans don't have to manually form-encode your POST data or add query strings to uniform resource locators (URLs). Requests allow you to add content like parameters, form data, headers, and multipart files through simple Python libraries. It also permits you to access the response data of Python.

One can use tarball, pip or easy_installl to install the request library. Adding the code, import request, at the beginning of your script allows you to import the appropriate module. You can make a request when you ping a portal or a website for information. Requests decode any content that gets pulled from a server. The Request library guesses about encoding the response when one makes a request to the server based on the HTTP header.

Scrapy

It is accessible for Python 2.6+ and Python 3 and works on Windows, Linus, BSD, and Mac OSX. It is open-source and has a library. It is a Python framework that provides users with a complete package for developers with no worries about maintain code. Web scraping is a crucial tool for data science because it gets information from the web that helps in analysis and decision making.

The scrappy command-line tool controls scrapy. The command-line tool provides commands for several reasons. These commands include global commands such as shell, fetch, view, version, and genspinder. Global commands play their roles without an active scrapy project.

There are also project-specific commands such as check, bench, edit, and list. They work function inside a scrapy project.

Pendulum

It is a Python package that eases datetimes manipulation. It gives classes that are drop-in replacements for the former classes. The following are methods that are used to create new DateTime instance:

- The no() method.
- The DateTime() if it's not specified it sets the time to 00:00:00.
- The instance() function that helps in inheriting a DateTime instance.
- The from_format() utilizes custom tokens to come up with a DateTime focus.

Pyflux

It gets used in prediction and time series analysis. It has a wide range of flexible array of interference options(Bayesian and frequent). You can build a full probabilistic model where latent variables and data act as random variables through joint probability. The probabilistic approach is vital for time series tasks such as forecasting because it provides a complete picture of uncertainty.

The PyFlux API is created to be as clear as possible. The following steps get used in the model building process:

Creating a model instance. The main arguments here are a family that highlights the distribution of modeled time series such as poison distribution. Data input such as a pandas data frame and design functions such as autoregressive lags for an ARIMA model get used.

Secondly, there is prior formation which is associated with clarifying a family for every latent variable in the model using the adjust_prior method. When you print the latent variables attached to the model, you can view the latent variables. When the user intends to do the Maximum Likelihood, prior information can get ignored.

They fit a model. This involves specifying an interference option and using the fit method. The possibilities for this include black box variation interference (BBVI), maximum likelihood (MLE) and Metropolis-Hastings (M-H). The user is allowed to proceed to the post fitting methods once the interference options are complete. It enables the latent variable information to be updated.

The last step is model retrospection, evaluation, and prediction. The user can criticize with posterior predictive checks, look at historical fit, and do a range of related tasks for their model once a model has been correctly fitted.

Arrow

This library provides a sensible and human- friendly approach to formatting, manipulating, creating, and converting dates, timestamps and time. It plugs gaps in functionality, updates, executes DateTime type, and provides an intelligent module application programming interface (API) which allows common creation scenarios. It helps merely programmers work deal with times and dates with fewer imports and less code.

Arrow contains the following features:

- Massive support for ISO 8601.

- Contain shift method which supports relative offsets such as weeks.
- It supports Python 2.7.3.6, 3.5, 3.8, and 3.7.
- By default, it is aware of timezone and UTC.
- It parses and parses strings automatically.
- It contains a fully-implemented drop-in replacement for DateTime.
- It allows access to simple creation options for many standard input scenarios.
- It converts time zones.
- Supports and humanizes a growing list of contributed locales.
- It generates floors, ranges, periods, and ceilings for time frames ranging from microsecond to a year.
- It allows an extension for your arrow derived types.

IPython

IPython is an open-source library. IPython supports Python 3.3 and 2.7 or newer. It provides several features such as interactive data visualization and the use of graphic user interface (GUI) toolkits. It provides a browser-based notebook interface that supports text, code, inline plots, and mathematical expressions. It also has interactive shells that are either Qt-based or terminal. The Python interactive shells have the following features:

- Session reloading and logging.
- It allows access to the system shell with a user-extensible alias system.
- You can access the Python profiler and PDB debugger.
- It helps in extensive syntax processing for special purpose situations.
- It has a comprehensive object into a spectrum.
- It has a rich configuration that contains easy switching between different setups.
- With automatically generated references, there is caching of output results.
- It inputs history persistently across all sessions.

The command-line interface takes after the above functionality and also includes the adds below:

- Allows integration with a command-line editor for a better workflow.
- It highlights syntax as you type.
- There is real multi-line editing.

Imbalanced Learn

It supports Python 3.6+. It is a Python library that offers several ways of re-sampling techniques in datasets that show a strong between-class imbalance. It is a part of scikit-learn-contrib and scikit-learn projects. The library can get used in a scientific publication. Large skewed data sets are more common. Here, the minority outnumbered by one or more classes. This issue can be solved by re-sampling the dataset. It offsets this imbalance, hence getting to a fair decision boundary. Re-sampling methods can get divided into the following categories:

- Over-sampling the minority class. Methods of oversampling are Synthetic Minority over Sampling Technique, Support Vectors SMOTE, and random minority over-sampling technique.
- Under-sampling majority class which involves Instance Hardness Threshhhold, One-Sided Selection, under-sampling with Cluster Centroids, and Neighbourhood Cleaning Rule.
- Combining the under- and oversampling.
- Creating ensemble balanced sets.

TensorFlow

It is a Python library created and maintained by Google and displayed under the Apache 2.0 open source license. It gets used for quick numerical computing designed and released by Google. It is a grassroots library that is often used to create deep learning models by utilizing wrapper libraries or directly. Examples in TensorFlow are:

- An operation is a given abstract computation that takes input attributes and gives output attributes.
- Nodes do computations and contain zero or more inputs. Tensor is data that moves in between nodes.
- Edges are used to synchronize behavior within the graph. Graphs explain the flow of data, looping, branching, and updates.

Use Cases of TensorFlow

Image recognition. The primary purpose is to note and identify people and objects in images. It gets used in healthcare industries, social media, and handset manufacturing companies.

Text summarization can be learned with a technique known as sequence-to-sequence learning which gets used to provide headlines for news.

Time series. Here, TensorFlow time series algorithms analyze time series data to extract useful statistics. To generate alternative versions of time series, TensorFlow allows predicting of non-specific periods.

Sound recognition. This can be in the form of flaw detection, voice search, voice recognition, and sentiment analysis. Neural networks can understand audio signals when adequately fed with data.

Video detection gets used in airports, gaming, and security fields. TensorFlow neural networks work on video data.

Pytorch

It is a learning library that is an open-source library that utilizes graphics processing units for applications like natural language processing. Facebook's artificial intelligence research group builds it. It is used for deep learning models because:

- It supports Python because it integrates with Python easily.
- It allows the use of an application programming interface (API).

- It provides a framework to create dynamic computational graphs and even alters them during runtime.

PyTorch makes an imperative paradigm where each line of code needed to create a graph defines a part of that graph. The main elements of PyTorch are:

- It provides you with mathematical operations such as matrix operations.
- Optimum that gets used in creating several optimization algorithms that get utilized when building neural networks.
- It has PyTorch Tensors that can be used on a GPU and contain multi-dimensional arrays.
- An nn module is a group of modules that have trainable weights and produces output from input.

Caffe2

It is a learning framework that is scalable, lightweight, and modular. Caffe2 provides a straightforward and easy method for developers to interact with deep learning. You must install caffe2 so that you can work with it. It has the principles below:

- The openness which provides scientific progress calls for reference models, standard code, and reproductivity.
- It has a high speed for a lot of data processing.
- It has a community of developers that are involved in startup prototypes, academic research, and industrial application.
- It is very flexible as it allows new settings and tasks to be incorporated.

Zappa

It allows hosting of Python web apps without servers. It is a microframework for amazon web services (AWS). It eases the work of programmers because of its nature since there is no more payment for server uptime. One does not need to worry about keeping servers online, and there is no web server configuration to be done. It has hacks that permit it to work:

- No way allows the setting of headers; thus, it turns cookie setting 301/302 responses into 200 responses.
- You can only map one kind of cookie. To allow this Zappa packages multiple codes into a single code.

- It turns vertical turret lathe(VTL) into a web server gateway interface(WSGI) to allow mapping of headers, method, bodies query strings, and params.
- It attaches response codes to response bodies, uses base 64 to encode and decode things, and maps the reply to those bodies.

Pipenv

It uses virtualnv, the good old requirement txt, and pip for solving problems for general workflow. It simplifies and integrates the creation process to a single line of the command-line tool. It has the features below:

- If .env files exist, it loads them with ease.
- It generates a Pipfile if it does not exist.
- It specifies what the programmer wants by enabling deterministic builds.
- By searching for a Pipefile, it finds the home of your project
- It comes up with a virtualenv in a standard location
- When pyenv is available, it installs required Python.

- It creates and confirms file lashes for locked dependencies.

The main commands in Pipfile are a lock, uninstall, and install. The other commands include check which confirms security vulnerabilities. The run command allows the running of commands that come from a virtual environment. Graph command shows a dependency graph that belongs to the installed dependencies.

Flashtext

It is specially created for the reason of searching and replacing words in a document. When searching keywords, FlashText returns keywords that are found in the string. FlashText creates a new string with keywords in the case of replacing. Theses actions happen in a single pass. FlashText provides solutions very fast. Searching happens in two ways. The methods that have a loop run n times. N is the number of words in the keyword. The loop in the other method runs m times. M is the word in the sample. Checking a key is faster than checking a word in a string.

Dash

It can get written on top of React.js, plotly.js, and flask. It is a framework in Python that creates analytical web applications. It gets used for visualization, instrument control, reporting, data analysis, and data exploration. Dash callbacks make dash apps interactive. Callbacks are Python functions that get called when an input component's property changes. It has component libraries which include:

- The Dash DataTable allows you to interact with it. It supports editing, sorting, filtering, styling, and conditional formatting.
- Data Canvas which are annotations and drawings get used for processing of images.
- Dash Cure Components has a set of higher-level components such as tables, dropdowns, sliders, and graphs.
- Dash HTNL Components which provide HTML tags and explains how they work.
- Dash Bio Components get used for visualizing bioinformatics data.
- Dash Cytoscape which creates interactive, customizable, and reactive graphs.

Pandas

It is used for machine learning and artificial intelligence. It is a Berkeley Source Distribution (BBSD) licensed, an open-source library that provides secure data structures, high-performance, and data analysis tools for the Python programming language. Programmers do not need to switch to domain-specific language such as R when doing data analysis. Pandas search in scikit-learn and statmodels for them to implement significant modeling functionality outside panel and linear regression. It has the following features:

- Flexible pivoting and reshaping datasets.
- It allows columns to be deleted and inserted to perform size mutability from data structures.
- It contains high performance joining and merging of datasets.
- Data manipulation and integrated indexing are done using a fast and integrated data frame.
- It performs intelligent label-based fancy indexing, slicing, and subsetting of large data.
- Easy manipulation of disorganized data into an orderly form can be done by data alignment and integrated handling of missing data.

- It contains tools for writing and reading data between in-memory different formats and data structures such as Microsoft Excel, SQL databases, and CSV.
- It is highly optimized for performance and has critical paths written in the C programming language.
- It contains hierarchical axis indexing that allows a way of working with high-dimensional data in a much lower-dimensional data structure.

Keras

It is a Python library that is open source, written for machine running, and constructing neural network projects. It executes graphics processing units (GPUs) and central processing units (CPUs) once given the underlying framework. It runs on Python 3.5 or 2.7. It was developed by Francois Chollet using the following guiding principles:

1. Minimalism: The library provides enough to achieve a result. It does not maximize readability.
2. Modularity: A model can be comprehended as a graph or a sequence.

3. Python is the only language that is being used for model files with custom file formats.
4. Extensibility: You can easily add new components to use within the framework.

Keras library gets used in learning models. The sequence model is the primary type of model, which is a linear stack of layers. Once you create a sequence, you can add layers to it in the order that you wish to perform computations. The following are steps used in creating a model:

- First, define the model you want to create.
- Compile the model by specifying loss function and optimizers.
- Fit the model. This is done by executing the model using data.
- Use the models to create predictions on new data.

Seaborn Python

It is based on matplotlib and gets used for data visualization. It allows access to a high-level interface for informative statistical and drawing attractive graphics. It offers the following functions:

- It provides useful views on the overall structure of hard datasets.
- It has clear dominance over matplotlib figure styling.
- It contains tools for selecting color palettes that show patterns in your data.
- It uses categorical variables to display aggregate statistics and observations.
- It contains options for visualizing bivariate or univariate distribution and compare them between data subsets.

You can quickly build complex visualizations using high-level abstractions for structuring multi-plot grinds.

One can either use built-in data sets that the library has or load a pandas data frame when working with seaborn. To use an integrated seaborn dataset, one can use the load_dataset function. This function makes it easy to document seaborn without getting mixed by things. Datasets change with time if they are not useful for seaborn documentation. However, when working with your data, seaborn works best with pandas arrays and data frames.

Chapter 9: Projects and Exercise in SQL Programming that Aid Python Coding

Now it is time for us to take a look at some of the different exercises that we are able to do when it comes to Python databases. This database project is going to help a developer in Python learn how to work with database programming and increase the skills that they have. We are also going to spend some time doing the CRUD operations in the database along with transaction management and some techniques of error-handling.

The first exercise that we are going to work with is handling a Hospital Information System. In this exercise, we are going to implement this kind of system. We are going to use two SQL tables to make it happen, the Doctor and the Hospital. The query that we do in SQL is going to help us to prepare the tables that we need. The solution that is provided at the end of each question will help us to see what is going on, but it is best to try and solve the questions on your own so that we can learn along the way.

So first we need to make sure that we re doing the right queries in SQL to make sure that we can prepare the data and get the tables ready to go. We are going to create a table and use the INSERT query which is going to prepare a required data for us so that we are able to start the exercise. Note, remember that we are using these queries and testing them with MySQL. You are able to update per the requirements of the database server.

the first step that we will do here is create our database. The coding that we need to make this happen is going to be below:

CREATE database python_db;

Then we need to create our first table. We will create the Hospital Table first before working on the second one:

CREATE TABLE `python_db`.`Hospital` (
`Hospital_Id` INT UNSIGNED NOT NULL ,
`Hospital_Name` TEXT NOT NULL , `Bed_Count` INT ,
PRIMARY KEY (`Hospital_Id`)) INSERT INTO `hospital`
(`Hospital_Id`, `Hospital_Name`, `Bed Count`)
VALUES ('1', 'Mayo Clinic', '200'), ('2', 'Cleveland
Clinic', '400'), ('3', 'Johns Hopkins', '1000'), ('4', 'UCLA
Medical Center', '1500')

The second thing that we are able to do is make sure that we go through and create the table for Doctor like we needed before. The coding that we need to make this one happen is going to be below:

CREATE TABLE `python_db`.`Doctor` (`Doctor_Id` INT UNSIGNED NOT NULL , `Doctor_Name` TEXT NOT NULL , `Hospital_Id` INT NOT NULL , `Joining_Date` DATE NOT NULL , `Speciality` TEXT NULL , `Salary` INT NULL , `Experience` INT NULL , PRIMARY KEY (`Doctor_Id`)) INSERT INTO `doctor` (`Doctor_Id`, `Doctor_Name`, `Hospital_Id`, `Joining_Date`, `Speciality`, `Salary`, `Experience`) VALUES ('101', 'David', '1', '2005-2-10', 'Pediatric', '40000', NULL), ('102', 'Michael', '1', '2018-07-23', 'Oncologist', '20000', NULL), ('103', 'Susan', '2', '2016-05-19', 'Garnacologist', '25000', NULL), ('104', 'Robert', '2', '2017-12-28', 'Pediatric ', '28000', NULL), ('105', 'Linda', '3', '2004-06-04', 'Garnacologist', '42000', NULL), ('106', 'William', '3', '2012-09-11', 'Dermatologist', '30000', NULL), ('107', 'Richard', '4', '2014-08-21', 'Garnacologist', '32000', NULL), ('108', 'Karen', '4', '2011-10-17', 'Radiologist', '30000', NULL)

Now that we have the tables ready to go for us, it is time to dive in and answer some of the questions that we need so that we can handle some of the exercises that we are doing here. The first question that we want to work with is to connect ourselves to the database and then print out the version that will come with it. We are able to do this with the help of implementing the functionality to help connect to the database and print out the version. The coding that we are going to need to ensure that we can connect over to our database is going to be below:

def getDbConnection(): #code to Get Database connection def closeDbConnection(connection): #Code Close Database connection def readDbVersion(): # Execute SQL query to print database server version print("Start of a Python Database Programming Exercise\n") readDbVersion() print("End of a Python Database Programming Exercise\n\n")

There are a few hints that we are able to work with here as well. These can include write SQL query in order to get the database server version. We can also connect to the database and use the cursor.execute() function to make it all execute the query for your needs. And then when we want to be able to fetch out the records that we are going to use, we will be able to use the function of cursor.fetchall() to get it to happen.

When all of this comes together, you will get the output that is below to help us out:

Start of a Python Database Programming Exercise Connected to MySQL database... MySQL Server version is 5.7.19 Your connected to - ('python_db',) End of a Python Database Programming Exercise

We are able to take this a bit further and work with the second question as well. this I where we are going to read the given hospital and doctor information that we have. This one is going to require that we are able to implement the functionality to help read out the details of a given doctor from the doctor table and then the hospital off that table as well. This means that we need to be able to read the records from the Hospital and Doctor Table as per given hospital ID and the Doctor ID and then display this information as you would like. The coding that we are able to use to make this one work will include the following:

def readHospitalDetails(hospital_Id): #Read data from Hospital table def readDoctorDetails(doctor_Id): # Read data from Doctor table print("Start of a Python Database Programming Exercise\n\n") readHospitalDetails(2) *readDoctorDetails(105) print("End of a Python Database Programming Exercise\n\n*

We are able to go through this and implement a bit of the functionality that we need in order to create a list of doctors. There are a few different methods that we are able to use for this one but in the code that we are going to work with, we are going to focus on the given Specialty that this doctor holds and the salary levels that end up being higher than the input amount that we are placing in. The code that we need to use to make this happen will be below:

def getSpecialistDoctorsList(Speciality, Salary): #Fetch doctor's details as per Speciality and Salary print("Start of a Python Database Programming Exercise\n\n") getSpecialistDoctorsList("Garnacologist", 30000) print("End of a Python Database Programming Exercise\n\n")

This is a simple code to work with, but now we want to make sure that we are seeing what the output of all that is going to be below:

Start of a Python Database Programming Exercise Printing Doctors record as per given Speciality Doctor Id:

= 105 Doctor Name: = Linda Hospital Id: = 3 Joining Date: = 2004-06-04 Speciality: = Garnacologist Salary: = 42000 Experience: = None Doctor Id: = 107 Doctor Name: = Richard Hospital Id: = 4 Joining Date: = 2014-08-21 Speciality: = Garnacologist Salary: = 32000 Experience: = None End of a Python Database Programming Exercise

Before we end out this chapter, we need to take a look at some of the hints that will make this one work a little bit before. First, remember that you need to be able to define the parameterized query. Then we need to use the function of cursor.execute() in order to get that query executed in time. And then we can use the same function that we talked about before in order to end the whole thing by fetching the results, and this is with the function of cursor.fetchall.

Of course, we have to remember that these are just a few of the things that you are able to do when it comes to working with Python and SQL together. These can show us just how simple some of the coding can end up being, once you get the hang of working with databases and putting the coding and the benefits of both of these languages to good use together.

Conclusion

Thank you for taking the time to read this guidebook! We hope that it was able to provide you with some of the resources and information that you need to handle Python, SQL, and the databases that are important to your business.

Learning how to program in the beginning can be hard. But when it is time to work with some of your own databases, and it is time to handle all of the different entries that are a part of your business, working with Python and SQL are going to be some of the best ways to get this started. When you are ready to make sure that you are getting the best out of these, this guidebook will be able to provide you with that assistance as well.

Many businesses need to work with databases to better serve their customers. When you are ready to get started, make sure to check out this guidebook and learn how Python and SQL can work together to make your database as strong and powerful as possible.